RULE

RULE
A PHILOSOPHICAL DIALOGUE

Nicholas J. Pappas

Algora Publishing
New York

Library of Congress Cataloging-in-Publication Data

Names: Pappas, Nicholas J., author.
Title: Rule : a philosophical dialogue / Nicholas J. Pappas.
Description: New York : Algora Publishing, [2023] | Summary: ""Rule" adopts
    the tradition of political philosophy begun by Socrates, refined by
    Xenophon and Plato. The book concentrates on something the characters
    call life-without-rule. What would that be? How does it differ from anarchy? What
makes it so appealing and what are the trade-offs? "— Provided by publisher.
Identifiers: LCCN 2023017753 (print) | LCCN 2023017754 (ebook) | ISBN
    9781628945126 (trade paperback) | ISBN 9781628945133 (hardcover) | ISBN
    9781628945140 (pdf)
Subjects: LCSH: Democracy—Philosophy. | Social control—Philosophy. | Rule
    of law—Philosophy. | Freedom—Philosophy. | Philosophy, Ancient.
Classification: LCC JC75.D36 P366 2023 (print) | LCC JC75.D36 (ebook) |
    DDC 321.8/01—dc23/eng/20230815
LC record available at https://lccn.loc.gov/2023017753
LC ebook record available at https://lccn.loc.gov/2023017754

More Books by Nick Pappas
from Algora Publishing

Controvert, or On the Lie and Other Philosophical Dialogues, 2008

Aristocrat, and The Community: Two Philosophical Dialogues, 2010

On Awareness: A Collection of Philosophical Dialogues, 2011

Belief and Integrity: Philosophical Dialogues, 2011

On Strength, 2012

On Freedom: A Philosophical Dialogue, 2014

On Life: Philosophical Dialogues, 2015

On Love: A Philosophical Dialogue, 2016

On Destiny: A Philosophical Dialogue, 2016

On Wisdom: A Philosophical Dialogue, 2017

All of Health: A Philosophical Dialogue, 2018

On Education: A Philosophical Dialogue, 2018

On Power: A Philosophical Dialogue, 2019

On Ideas: A Philosophical Dialogue, 2020

On Passivity: A Philosophical Dialogue, 2021

On Authority: A Philosophical Dialogue, 2021

On Violence: A Philosophical Dialogue, 2022

Looks: A Philosophical Dialogue, 2022

CHARACTERS: *Director, Student, Father*

SETTING: *Country club*

* * *

1

Father: How was your lunch?

Director: It was pretty good. But the view is better.

Father: That's how I always feel. I could sit up here all day and look down over the course. It's too bad you don't play, Director.

Director: They say golf is something that takes regular practice.

Father: I come here every night after work and drive a small bucket of balls. It only takes me fifteen minutes.

Student: I don't practice at all, Dad, and I still beat you every time.

Father: One day you'll understand that that's the sweetest defeat there is. No father minds losing to his son—no good father, anyway. So what were you two talking about when I came in? And I'm sorry again I was late.

Student: It's okay. I'm used to it. We were talking about my senior year elective.

Father: That politics course?

Student: Yes. 'Questioning Democracy'.

Father: It can't be any good with a title like that.

Student: Why not?

Father: Democracy is something we defend. You really shouldn't question here.

Student: Oh, but we do. You should hear the questions.

Father: What do they ask?

Student: If democracy isn't better replaced by anarchy.

Father: What? I'm paying a small fortune for you to attend that college and they're asking questions like that?

Student: Should we just believe in democracy unthinkingly?

Father: What's to think? Director, help me here.

Director: What's the old saying? 'Democracy is the worst form of government— except for all the others.'

Father: Ha, ha. And it's true.

Student: Absence of government is best.

Father: Oh, there's always some form of government. Even under anarchy some-one will rule.

Student: The laws of human nature will rule.

Father: How trusting youth is. Who says what these laws are?

Student: We hold them to be self-evident.

Father: I'm sure you do. Director, what did you say about all this before I arrived?

Director: I proposed that instead of going for anarchy, we might go for more democracy.

Father: What do you think of that, Son?

Student: Direct democracy, with no representatives and popular votes on all im-portant things, is the next step.

Father: But?

Student: But it's not even close to a substitute for anarchy in the end.

Father: Oh, what's the difference? Democracy in its purest form always becomes anarchy—in the end.

2

Student: I don't want direct democracy.

Director: Why not?

Student: There the people rule—through votes. I don't want any rule.

Father: Then who will talk sense to the people?

Student: What do you mean?

Father: To govern is to talk sense.

Student: When is the last time the people listened to sense?

Father: It happens every day.

Student: I know you don't believe that.

Father: Let me put it this way. In our government, leaders must resist the lack of sense.

Student: Really? When was the last time you saw a representative resist the popular will?

Director: Is there popular will in an anarchy?

Student: We talk about this a lot in class.

Director: Which side do you take?

Student: There's no popular will in anarchy.

Director: Why not?

Student: Popular will has to manifest itself some way. Our way is the vote. So what if we don't have votes?

Father: What people elect to do will be their vote.

Student: It's not the same thing.

Director: What's the difference?

Student: For one, voting involves false choice.

Father: What's false about choice? We organize our society through the choices we offer.

Student: I'm not in favor of that kind of organization.

Father: You're a friend of chaos?

Student: No, I'm not. I'm a friend of self-organization.

Father: I'd like to see how well self-organization keeps violent people in check.

Student: That always happens.

Director: What do you mean?

Student: People jump to violence right away. 'We must have rule or violence will reign.'

Father: What you call 'rule' is what unites decent people. You're not in favor of that?

Student: Why don't you ask me if I'm in favor of mom and apple pie?

Father: But you do admit that isolated people are weak, don't you?

Student: And now you'll tell me that banded together they're strong.

Father: They are.

Student: But at what cost?

Father: What do you mean?

Student: Our professor said the banding process kills important differences. It makes us all the same.

Father: Oh, we're not all the same.

Student: But differences not nurtured die.

Director: Does anarchy nurture differences?

Student: No.

Father: Then what's the point of anarchy?

Student: It allows us to nurture them ourselves—without the pressure of the popular, general will.

Father: Oh, we can nurture differences in our democracy.

Student: But only the strong succeed.

Father: That's life.

3

Director: What does it take for the weak to succeed in an anarchy?

Student: They just... succeed!

Father: With no police force to protect their rights?

Student: If we had a police force, it would be an imperfect anarchy.

Director: Would you say what we have now is an imperfect democracy?

Student: I would.

Father: And you really would prefer an imperfect anarchy to an imperfect democracy?

Student: Unless someone can show me why I shouldn't.

Director: Aside from allowing the weak to develop, what good comes of anarchy?

Student: That's like asking, 'Aside from allowing us to breathe, what good comes of oxygen?'

Director: You mentioned the pressure of the general will being absent in anarchy. What is the general will?

Student: It's just the collective will of the people, the people as a whole.

Director: And without this will as a whole, nurturing difference is possible for all?

Student: Yes.

Director: Father, are you in favor of the general will?

Father: Try winning a war without it.

Student: Yes, but I'm talking about global anarchy. There will be no wars.

Father: Son, this sounds like a wonderful dream. But it's a dream nonetheless. Who will be first to lay down his arms?

Student: I understand the difficulty. But assuming we can get there, let's talk about the benefits.

Father: That's like saying, 'Assuming we don't need money, let's talk about the benefits of not having to work.'

Student: Oh, it's not like that.

Director: What is it about the general will?

Student: It exerts a constant pressure on us, one that silences quiet voices.

Director: So the general will is a sort of loud noise?

Student: Of course it is. Think of political rallies. Nothing but noise.

Director: Why can't we nurture our quiet voices on our own?

Student: We grow when we communicate our quiet voices to others. If the others are listening to the noise of the general will, they can't hear.

Director: What makes people listen to the general will?

Student: Fear.

Father: Fear?

Student: People are afraid they'll be attacked if they don't heed the general will.

Director: You're not afraid?

Student: Sure I am. I'm afraid of attack dogs and wolves.

Father: What are you, a sheep?

Student: What's wrong with sheep? They band together for common defense.

Father: What they do I wouldn't call defense.

Student: And yet sheep are great adherents to the general will.

Director: Metaphors aside, do anarchists band together for defense?

Student: 'Band' is too strong a word.

Father: Then they're too weak to fight.

Director: Who will lead the defense?

Student: Natural leaders.

Father: And what will they lead? An army?

Student: No, no army. The populace will be armed, and will fight when it must.

4

Director: So anarchists aren't docile.

Student: They stand up for themselves.

Father: But how do you prevent that from turning into... anarchy?

Student: You mean chaos? We simply follow human nature's laws. There is no chaos here—unlike in democracy gone bad.

Father: But if a country dismantles its government, it opens itself to attack. That's one of nature's laws.

Student: Maybe it won't be the whole country.

Father: Then how will you protect yourself?

Student: From our former countrymen? Our former military might... admire us.

Father: And what, they'll protect you from themselves?

Student: Precisely.

Father: Ha! What will they admire? An army is the opposite of an anarchy!

Student: That's the point. They'll want anarchy, too.

Father: No, no, no. Militaries are wholly based on rule—on orders and chain of command.

Student: Why?

Father: Because that's what armies...are!

Student: But why?

Father: You want the bottom line? Because armies ask you to risk your life.

Student: For what?

Father: The country you defend!

Student: Anarchists are willing to defend what they have. And what they have is better.

Director: Who is the enemy?

Student: People who try to dominate others.

Director: And if these people win?

Student: The anarchy is dead.

Director: What does it become?

Student: In all likelihood? A tyranny.

Director: People often say that dying democracies become tyrannies.

Student: And you want to know if they become anarchies instead? They don't. Anarchy isn't some inevitable thing. It's a sought after state.

Director: Can a collapsing democracy save its people by choosing to become an anarchy?

Student: I think so.

Father: Do you think our democracy is collapsing today?

Student: I think it shows signs.

Father: So you think it's time to act.

5

Student: Would I like to see an anarchy form? Yes.

Director: To be sure, you're not talking about a situation where anything goes.

Student: Yes and no. No, we're not talking about Sodom and Gomorrah; yes, people will be free to realize their potential.

Father: Because there will be no general will. I don't understand that.

Student: The general will creates a pressure to conform.

Father: A little pressure here and there and you up and condemn democracy?

Student: A little pressure? Hundreds of millions of people and their expectations pressing on you, and that's a little pressure?

Father: Oh, you'd complain about the pressure in a town of population one hundred.

Student: The point is that all these people should live their lives as they see fit, without interference from some general will. Can't you imagine how that would be?

Father: I can—and that's why I object!

Student: You're afraid.

Father: Of course I'm afraid! You should be, too. Except that fool of a professor wants you to lose your common sense.

Student: That's exactly what he wants us to lose.

Father: Ha!

Student: No, really. He says the general will generates common sense.

Director: He wants you to have uncommon sense.

Student: Yes. He wants us to have our own sense. He wants us to develop our sense, to refine our sense, to live by our sense. Do democrats do that?

Father: Democrats know their salvation lies in each other. From many one. E pluribus unum. And when we are one, we are unstoppable.

Director: What does it mean to be one?

Father: We join together to pursue a goal.

Director: Victory in war, for instance?

Father: Yes, of course. But also victory in commerce.

Director: Victory? In commerce? Isn't commerce supposed to be a win-win affair?

Father: Well....

Director: When people engage in commerce, don't they sometimes make investments, form alliances, outside their country?

Father: You know they do.

Director: What's the effect of that?

Father: If taken too far? Lines of allegiance blur.

Director: Student, what are the lines of allegiance in an anarchy?

Father: The lines are personal only. I might have allegiance to you as a friend. But I don't have allegiance to a country.

Director: Father, is it possible that if lines of allegiance are blurred because of trade, anarchy might result?

Father: One line blurs, another is drawn.

Student: What does that mean?

Father: If trade is ascendent, allegiance will be to firms.

Director: Student, would anarchists have allegiance to their firms?

Student: I never thought about it before. I suppose they shouldn't.

Director: Why?

Student: Because firms are hierarchical.

Director: Do you think there can be anarchist firms?

Student: Now that I think of it, I don't see why not.

Father: You don't see why not? Human nature is why not! Or do you think greed and lust to rule go away with the government?

Student: Those things derive from ambition, and there's a difference between ambition and healthy ambition.

Director: What's the difference?

Student: Rule. Healthy ambition might strive to find a cure for a terrible disease. Unhealthy ambition strives to dominate others.

6

Director: Do you think some people by nature wish to dominate others?

Student: If they do they'll have a bad time in anarchy. Everyone will resist.

Director: And if not everyone resists?

Student: I suppose some will be dominated.

Director: And if dominated, ruled?

Student: Of course.

Director: Those who are ruled can't be anarchists, can they?

Student: No, they can't.

Director: What can be done?

Student: Anarchy depends on virtue, the virtue to resist. The only thing to be done is to foster more of that.

Father: Democrats have plenty of this virtue. Maybe you can borrow some from them.

Director: What sort of rule do democrats resist?

Father: Tyranny.

Director: Student, what sort of rule does anarchy resist?

Student: All sorts of rule, but especially tyranny.

Director: Anarchy and democracy have much in common. But what about other forms of government? Kingship, aristocracy. Don't they resist tyranny, too?

Student: I think they have to.

Director: Is there any form of government that doesn't resist tyranny?

Student: I don't think there is.

Director: So maybe the question is what form of government, given our circumstances, best fights tyranny.

Father: I agree. And that best form today is democracy.

Student: But maybe not for long.

Director: Father, how does democracy fight tyranny?

Father: Through freedom and the general will.

Student: You don't see a contradiction in that?

Father: I don't. The general will is the guardian of our freedom. We agree in general, and will into effect, that we have freedoms that cannot be taken away. Your anarchy will do the same.

Student: I don't think so. Anarchists don't have to will their freedoms into effect. They simply are in effect.

Director: Can these freedoms be taken away?

Student: If the anarchy collapses into tyranny, sure.

Director: How are they taken away in a democracy?

Student: Ask any minority.

Father: Not getting what you want in a vote is a far cry from having your freedoms taken away.

Student: It depends on the vote. More is at stake in some than others.

Father: I'm glad you recognize that fact. But you would have no votes. How do people get what they want?

Student: They negotiate solutions.

7

Director: What does it take for negotiations to go consistently well?

Student: A little faith in human nature.

Director: So anarchists must believe.

Student: Yes.

Director: What else must they believe?

Student: I think that's it.

Father: Well, it sounds like utopia to me. What happens if bunches of anarchists lose their faith?

Student: It all falls apart.

Director: Student, can you tell us more about anarchy's faith?

Student: It's a sort of basic trust in one another.

Father: If we could all trust one another, maybe we wouldn't need government. But that's just a dream. Besides, you can only trust those you know—and you can't know everyone.

Student: But you can. Our communities will be small.

Father: I thought you were talking on a global scale.

Student: A globe full of small communities.

Director: And those communities must trust one another from time to time.

Student: Yes. They'll get to know one another first.

Father: A grand experiment in trust.

Student: Democracy was an experiment. Why not make another in anarchy?

Director: I wonder. Is there a People in an anarchy?

Student: Well, there's no People. But there are people.

Father: What's wrong with a People?

Student: A People has a general will. People have their own individual wills.

Director: A People also has an identity.

Student: Anarchists have their own identities. Is it even possible for a person not to have an identity?

Father: Haven't you heard of an identity crisis?

Student: That's what happens when you've been living under a false identity and start to see the truth.

Director: Is The People a false identity?

Student: Yes.

Father: They teach you this in your class?

Student: I don't know that I'd say the professor teaches this. But we've had discussions about it.

Father: Ungrateful, that's what it is. This is the greatest country on Earth, the greatest ever—all because of The People.

Director: How were The People originally formed?

Father: They were the population at the time, brought together through crisis, revolt.

Director: And when that People died off?

Father: Then the People were those who lived by the lights of the Founders.

Director: Guided by the Constitution.

Father: And other documents, sure.

Director: Student, do you think your anarchists can do better than the Constitution?

Student: No. They wouldn't even try.

Director: Why not?

Student: The Constitution rules our land. Or it's supposed to rule our land.

Director: The People don't rule?

Student: We don't live in a true democracy. Yes, ultimately the People rule because they can vote to change or get rid of the Constitution. But for all practical purposes we live in a republic.

Director: And anarchists don't want a democracy, or a constitution, or a republic—or any of that—because it all involves rule.

Student: Exactly.

Father: Do anarchists want laws?

Student: No, no laws.

Father: So I can just walk up to someone and punch them in the nose?

Student: You'll suffer consequences for that without any law. And the knowledge of that will deter.

8

Father: What if my punching someone in the nose starts a generations long family feud? What do we do about that?

Student: Other families will step in and break it up.

Father: You'd be surprised how little families want to get involved in other families' troubles.

Student: You'd be surprised how much in an anarchy people care.

Father: Maybe. But tell me this. Families are institutions, with varying types of rule—will you do away with them?

Student: No. Families are a naturally occurring fact. But families won't have any type of rule.

Director: That's odd. I thought they might have more rule in an anarchy than now.

Student: Why would you think that?

Director: The authority of the family is held in check by the People today. It's subject to the laws.

Student: Of course.

Director: But in an anarchy, families are subject to nothing. So what's to stop families from growing tyrannical with their own?

Student: It's as it is with family feuds. People will step in and fight the tyranny.

Father: But what if they don't? What if the institution of the family grows so powerful that no one dares step in?

Student: I don't see how it could. Families grow tyrannical because something from the outside is wrong. In our anarchy, nothing like that will be wrong.

Father: You have a lot of faith in families.

Student: I do.

Director: So there are two faiths. Faith in human nature; faith in families.

Student: The two are of a piece.

Father: Our democracy shares these faiths, you know.

Student: Except when the government steps in.

Father: Let's go back to something. Do you really believe the problems in families come from some external factor?

Student: Let me give you an example. A man goes to work. He is abused at work. He comes home and in his frustration kicks his loving dog. Do you know what I mean?

Father: Of course I do. Everyone who has been abused at work knows what you mean. So, what? In an anarchy there's no abuse at work?

Student: There is less.

Father: Why?

Student: Because of the lessened pressure to conform.

Director: The absence of the general will.

Student: Right.

Director: Student, can you explain how pressure to conform leads to abuse?

Student: It's simple. When we're under pressure we feel stress. When we feel stress, we don't act like ourselves. Stress can make us cruel though we're by nature kind.

Director: So without the pressure to conform, less abuse?

Student: Definitely.

Director: Hmm. Now you're making me think.

Student: What are you thinking?

Director: Who feels the pressure imposed by the general will?

Student: What do you mean? Everyone.

Director: I don't think so. The majority component of the general will feels good about this will. No?

Student: It's the minority who feel the pressure?

Director: Yes, I think so. What do you think?

Student: I think you have a point. That's what's great about anarchies. There is no majority or minority.

Father: What? Of course there is! There is always a majority and a minority.

Student: Even if that were true, the majority doesn't operate with the force of law.

Director: What's wrong with the force of law?

Student: It amplifies one side of the argument beyond its natural strength.

Father: I would argue the contrary. Natural strength is tempered by the law.

Director: Natural strength is rendered predictable by the law.

Father: That's a good point. Minorities should be grateful for law.

Student: Ha! Predictable gloom is what that brings.

Father: How would you have it?

Student: Nothing is more open and free than a self-regulating community beyond the reach of law.

Father: I'll grant you that may be. But I will tell you this. Nothing is more fleeting.

9

Student: The pleasure of a wonderful meal is fleeting. Does that mean we shouldn't eat?

Father: You would have your anarchy if only for a while?

Student: Yes. It might be an example that shines on for many, many years.

Father: Our democracy is an example that will, no doubt, shine on for many, many years.

Student: And this is good. Democracy is the next best thing.

Father: Democracy is the only realistic thing.

Student: People didn't agree when our democracy was born. Many didn't think it was realistic at all.

Father: And they were wrong.

Student: How?

Father: What do you mean? Look at our success. Freedom, wealth, power. What more could you want?

Student: For the freedom, wealth, and power to be more equally shared.

Director: Do anarchists believe in equality?

Student: No. Anarchists live equality.

Director: Why?

Student: What do you mean, 'Why?'

Director: What does it mean to live equality? And why would you?

Student: It means to respect each person as a unique living soul. And why would you do that? Because it's the truth.

Father: Then why not respect each dog and cat as a unique living soul?

Student: We should.

Father: So anarchy transcends the human?

Student: Yes. The ancient Athenians weren't even anarchists and yet they used to joke that donkeys might as well have been citizens, too.

Director: Who is human?

Student: Excuse me?

Director: Who deserves to be treated as human?

Student: Everyone does.

Director: Every dog and cat?

Student: They should be treated as unique living souls, but not human souls.

Director: What makes a soul human? The fact that it resides in a human form?

Student: Well, that doesn't sound so good.

Director: Why not?

Student: Because....

Father: Ha, ha! The anarchist is stuck! How can an anarchy rely on trust in human nature if it can't even say what a human is?

Student: The human might evolve.

Director: Into what?

Student: Shapes beyond our current conception.

Father: Science.

Director: Can you say more?

Father: Science is leading us down a certain path.

Director: Where the shape of humans will be changed?

Student: Yes, Director. But it won't happen all at once.

Director: Why not?

Student: People need their reference points.

Director: Two arms, two legs....

Student: Right.

Director: Why do you think that is?

Student: Because people don't know the essence of the human. They need the old bodily form.

Director: But you could do without that form.

Student: I could, and can.

Father: So it's anarchy in bodily form?

Student: Eventually? Why not? The form isn't what counts. It's the essence.

Father: But the essence is, at least in part, shaped by the form.

10

Director: Student, what's the human essence?

Student: The undefined.

Director: And that's why anarchy is the way?

Student: Yes. It allows the undefined to take whatever shape it may. There will be very many beautiful forms under anarchy, Director.

Father: If the anarchy isn't crushed by foreign powers.

Student: Communities of anarchists will look out for each other. They'll defend their trusted and valued neighbors.

Father: I guess I just don't have enough trust.

Student: You would if you got to know people clearly without the fog of the general will.

Father: That may be. But tell me why it's a fog.

Student: Because when you conform, you compromise your judgment.

Father: Judgment about my neighbors.

Student: Yes. Instead of seeing them for what they are, you see them through the lens of the general will.

Director: Why is the lens of the general will bad?

Student: Because nothing is true. Everything is average, the average of millions and millions of individual wills. That average can be very powerful; but it doesn't help you in seeing someone who is right before your eyes.

Father: So in anarchy everything is only what's before your eyes.

Student: Yes. Everything is only what it is. Does that make sense?

Father: I think it does. But don't you think there are people in democracies who see things that way?

Student: I'm sure there are. But they have to fight against the general will.

Director: Are you saying there is no fight in anarchies?

Student: No, there is very much a fight. Everything depends on seeing things for what they are. In a democracy and its general will, you can rest on that will. There is no such rest for the anarchist. It's a constant effort of coming to see.

Father: That sounds tiring.

Student: Tiring, sure. But when you see you're refreshed.

Father: And what about the lazy?

Student: Those who refuse to see? But who would refuse to see?

Father: Ha, ha.

Student: Seriously. Everyone makes the effort to see in an anarchy.

Father: There's no choice?

Student: It's simply human nature.

11

Director: But supposing people don't see, will the anarchy collapse?

Student: You mean if humans aren't human? Sure.

Director: So it's in everyone's interest to stir each other to see.

Student: Yes.

Director: Then in anarchy there's a place for philosophy.

Student: There definitely is—maybe more so than in any other community!

Director: Well, I'm relieved. But, really—more so than anywhere else?

Student: Maybe. Anarchy depends on clear thinking.

Father: And democracy doesn't?

Student: Democrats are taught to fall back on the general will. Anarchists have no such support.

Director: Anarchists operate without a net.

Father: What's wrong with having a net?

Student: It always comes at a cost. In this case, freedom.

Father: What if I say we can have freedom without a net in a democracy, too?

Student: How?

Father: We ignore the general will.

Student: I think that's possible for rare thinkers. But the population as a whole? No way. It's hard to escape popular thought.

Father: But what happens when those who can't escape popular thought find themselves in an anarchy? They'll look for and find popular thought.

Student: I don't think they will. There is no 'popular thought' in an anarchy.

Director: Why not?

Student: Because anarchists are always breaking clumps of thought up before they harden.

Director: Anarchists, or philosophers?

Student: Anarchic philosophers.

Director: Will this be the first actual society in which philosophers have an established role?

Student: I think it might be. Philosophers are anarchists par excellence.

Director: Now I'm having doubts.

Student: Why?

Director: Every member of the society should play this role, not just philosophers.

Student: I see nothing wrong with that.

Director: Yes. But if everyone is a philosopher, no one is a philosopher. Do you agree?

Student: No, I don't. Why can't everyone be a philosopher? Maybe that's what anarchy is all about. Do you think everyone can be a philosopher in a democracy?

Father: Why not? Democracy, too, depends on thought—if only in forming a good general will. If all democratic citizens were philosophers, the general will would reflect this—and be sound.

Director: What do you think, Student?

Student: Philosophers aren't concerned with general anything. They take the general and break it down into particulars.

Father: That's not what philosophy does. Haven't you read any philosophers? They're very much concerned with the general. Some would even say they shape our general ideas themselves!

Director: Philosophers aside, what about demagogues? Are there any in an anarchy?

Student: No, there aren't. That's not to say some won't try. But if the people are clear headed, which they'll tend to be without the general will to cloud their view, the demagogues won't get far.

Father: Why do you think it's only the general will that clouds the view?

Student: There are other ways to cloud. But here's the thing. If your view is clouded, others can point this out. If your view is clouded and backed by the general will, who dares to point this out? Worse, who will listen?

Father: I don't believe the general will always clouds. Many in democracies think clear thoughts. Add that all up, and the general will is by and large clear.

Student: By-and-large-clear is worse than clouded.

Father: How so?

Student: Something close to the truth is always more misleading than something far from the truth.

Director: Well, there's truth in that. So are you saying democrats are, at best, a little bit off from truth?

Student: Yes. Which is why it's so hard to argue for anarchy with democrats.

Father: Oh, now you're being ridiculous. Who else would even hear these arguments? Monarchs? Aristocrats? Oligarchs? Tyrants?

Student: I'll give credit where credit is due. But democrats think they know best.

Father: They think that less than in any other sort of regime.

Director: What makes them doubt themselves?

Father: They have a suspicion.

Director: What suspicion?

Father: That they might be happier if they were king, or an aristocrat, and so on.

Director: And kings never think they might be happier as democrats?

Father: Who knows? People think strange things.

Director: But because democrats have this doubt, they're open to hearing of anarchy?

Father: They are open to hearing of a potentially happier state. Look at me. I'm a firm republican democrat. And here I am talking about anarchy. There are those, you know, who would shut this conversation down at once.

Director: I do know. And you're right. Hmm. 'Anarchy' is such a loaded word. Maybe we should say 'life-without-rule' instead.

Student: That's fine with me. 'Life-without-rule' comes without prejudice.

Director: Just as life-without-rule itself will be without prejudice?

Student: As free of prejudice as can be.

Director: What are the prejudices of democracy?

Student: We've been talking about the biggest. The value of the general will. People believe the general will is the best way of getting at the truth, or at the best policy.

Father: The best policy for the greatest number.

Student: Right. That's the effectual truth for a democrat. But what if there are policies that are even better for a smaller subset of the whole?

Father: Democrats won't believe it. What's best for most is best for all.

Director: Even though that's not strictly speaking true. What other prejudices do democrats have?

Father: We've said enough about that. What are the prejudices of life-without-rule?

Student: There are none.

Father: Oh, come on. Don't be such a partisan.

Student: No, really. There aren't. Prejudice is a function of rule.

Father: That's ridiculous. In your life-without-rule there will be prejudice, I'm sure.

Student: Where will it come from?

Father: We said families will hold much sway. They will be hot houses of prejudice.

Student: Only if they exercise rule within.

Director: If they do, what's to be done?

Student: Others must resist on behalf of those who can't.

Father: How would they resist? Dismantle the family? I think it's more likely they'd say, 'Oh, so-and-so's family is crazy. What can you do?'

Student: They wouldn't say that because they can see a real negative effect on their community. The community, without rule, is very much worth a fight.

Father: And with rule it's not?

Student: It is. But the general will gets in the way.

13

Father: How?

Student: If a few families here and there seem bad, even very bad, the general will can still seem good, lending a rosy color to everything in sight. Why not just let things be?

Director: Life-without-rule has a clearer view?

Student: Yes. Every kind of rule colors or distorts.

Director: So democrats might think things are fine even though there's very real trouble at hand.

Student: Right. And I'm not saying democrats don't care and don't many times take action, even heroic action, to make things right. But there's a certain tendency.

Father: And you think that makes it bad.

Student: Yes—but I think worse. It's sometimes malevolent.

Father: The majority?

Student: That's right.

Director: Can the majority know it's become malevolent?

Student: I don't think it would see itself that way. It might know it's angry and so on. But would it think it's bad? I doubt it.

Director: But a minority might know what the majority has become.

Student: Certainly.

Director: What can a minority do?

Student: In other times it might have called on outside powers to help.

Father: Help establish them in rule? That could never happen here. No outside power is strong enough for that.

Director: What if the minority is very rich?

Student: They could seek to challenge the general will from within.

Director: You mean they would seek to break up the general will.

Student: And become life-without-rule, yes.

Director: You don't think they'd establish an oligarchy or some other like form of rule?

Student: We might get lucky. They'd probably want, at first, what you suggest. But the majority won't have it. If the military sides with the majority in this, but agrees there is a problem with the general will, it might let neither rule.

Father: Why not take up rule itself under notions of emergency power?

Student: That might very well happen, and then become permanent. But there just might be enough respect for civilian life to make them hesitate here.

Director: So a society without-rule could come into being next to a colossal military that is emphatically with-rule within.

Father: An impossible dream.

Director: Tell us, Student. Do you think the military could ever be without rule?

Student: Well, they're asked to kill or die. So let me ask you this. What's more powerful, all things equal—a force that doesn't need to be forced to kill or die, or a force that does?

Father: The force that doesn't need coercion.

Student: What might make them act?

Father: Love.

Student: For what?

Father: That which they defend.

Student: So, what if soldiers bordering an anarchy love what they see? What if they love the society without rule? What if they'd be willing to defend it with their lives?

Director: Are you suggesting they might serve as volunteers?

Student: Yes. The professional military might dissolve.

Father: Again, we're talking in dreams. Do you have any idea what this dissolving would mean? Besides, no volunteer force can compete with a professional army.

Student: Not even if the volunteers outnumbered the old professional force by a factor of ten?

Father: Everyone would want to help? Maybe. But how would we coordinate this force?

Student: People would know what needs to be done—and they would do it.

Father: It's not that simple. But tell us. Who would they look to in a crisis?

Student: Natural leaders, of course.

Father: And those leaders won't compete?

Student: Natural leaders don't long to rule. They're simply willing to do so when needed.

Director: We'd have leadership but no rule.

Student: Yes. There would be no orders. Only reasoned explanations of what needs to be done.

Father: And when fear of death overrules sense in those who must do?

Student: That might happen. But not as often as you think. People have to be willing to defend what they have—assuming what they have is very, very good. And life-without-rule is that.

14

Father: But you're not saying life-without-rule eliminates fear of death.

Student: Many fears disappear when we can see things as they are.

Father: No way. Fear of death is a universal fear.

Student: Does it have to be? Maybe there was a time when people weren't afraid of death. But over the centuries, as they were ruled, they feared cutting short lives that hadn't really been lived.

Director: Rule as the smotherer of life.

Student: Yes. And who wants to smother life?

Director: Then why does it happen?

Student: Because of the oldest lie there is.

Father: What lie?

Student: That life is a rule-or-be-ruled affair.

Father: Why is that a lie?

Student: It's a false choice. It ignores the third possibility here—life-without-rule, our natural state.

Father: If that's our state of nature, it's a state that's quickly crushed.

Student: I don't deny that's what almost always happens. But imagine if it weren't. When we're born, for that first split second, we find ourselves in the world without rule. I believe we never forget that taste of life, no matter what follows. It haunts us in our dreams. It's why we're dissatisfied with how things are. We know there's better. So what if some of us start talking, start trying to wake people to the truth, the truth that life-without-rule is how we were meant to be? Imagine what's possible here.

Director: I'm trying to imagine, and I must confess I'm seeing some very good things. But help me understand what the downside is to life-without-rule. Surely it's not a perfect state.

Student: But it is. It has to be—because otherwise rule keeps slipping in. Imperfect anarchy can't protect itself as we'd like. It would require rule to do so, defeating the purpose of the whole thing.

Father: So imperfect anarchy is weak.

Student: It's tolerant—to a fault.

Director: Tolerant of rule?

Student: What can I say? Imperfect anarchists don't resist as much as they should.

Father: Why not err on the side of intolerance?

Student: Because intolerance is akin to rule.

Director: How?

Student: Who says what will or won't be tolerated? Someone who rules.

Father: Yes, Son, that makes sense. But I know you. You want more than tolerance. You want love.

Student: I.... Yes.

Director: Did I miss something here?

Father: He's talking about a society where everyone must love one another.

Student: Love as friends, yes.

Director: What's wrong with that?

Father: It's a dream! A whole society can't love each other as friends.

Student: Why not? Think about it. Without the friction of the general will rubbing against our souls, friendships never before possible will flourish!

Father: Before democracy there was no general will. Were people all friends then?

Student: Maybe. We really don't know.

Father: There is evidence of warfare going back as far as we can see.

Student: Maybe it was life-without-rule fighting aggressive rule, a rule driven by general will. I think we can make a case that the general will has always existed, to some degree, within all types of rule. Even tyrants must fight against the general will. Kings have to woo it. And so on.

Director: But democracy is the culmination of the general will and therefore of the types of rule?

Student: Yes. But I think we're headed for a time against all rule. The great battles of the future won't be against nation states. The great battles will be for the freedom of life-without-rule.

15

Father: What kind of battles are we talking about? Employees trying to free themselves from managers?

Student: I think you're teasing, but yes. They will listen to managers, but they won't obey.

Director: Are you saying that when life-without-rule comes, everyone in workplaces will listen to reason and do what must be done?

Student: Yes.

Father: And in this dream no one will be lazy or think too highly of themselves.

Student: I submit that laziness and self-importance derive, ultimately, from the problems of rule. Take those problems away and people will work to serve their interests within their proper spheres.

Director: These problems of rule are pervasive.

Student: They really are.

Director: Whence rule?

Student: I honestly don't know. Maybe it all started with an innocent mistake.

Director: Someone thought they knew better and enforced their will on others?

Student: For the benefit of those others? Sure, something like that. And then rule picked up momentum and grew into a terrible force.

Father: Do you have any idea what kind of luck it would take to create the conditions that would end all rule?

Student: I do. But even if we can't get one hundred percent of the way there, some is better than none.

Father: But is it? What if we weaken our society by having some life-without-rule, weaken it so that outside forces attack?

Student: That won't happen.

Father: Why not?

Student: Because life-without-rule is stronger than rule.

Director: How?

Student: People in life-without-rule organize themselves according to nature. They are properly aligned; thus they are stronger. Nature always trumps rule.

Father: Then why don't we see spontaneous life-without-rule movements arising against the general will?

Student: The general will is very strong, and people are afraid. They hear the word 'anarchy' and they think it can't be right. And so they shy away and submit.

Director: So anarchy has a public relations problem?

Student: Of the worst sort. That's why I think it's best to call it life-without-rule.

Father: How does life-without-rule proceed?

Student: It requires a certain critical mass of people who can shake off rule. I suspect this would have to happen by means of a happy accident.

Father: Happy accidents and dreams. I think that's all you've got. But give us an example.

Student: I... can't. Director?

Director: Rule would have to somehow be suspended. People would get a taste of freedom. They might remember that moment of freedom at birth that you were talking about. And somehow it might all make sense.

Father: How would rule be suspended?

Director: Oh, I don't know. Maybe one day government, or even rule in general, is wholly dependent on the internet. And let's say somehow it goes down for a long stretch of time. That might create a space, a space without rule.

Father: But none of the habits of rule would die. For that to happen it would take so much more.

Director: Well, that's the thing. Only some could make the leap. Student, do you see a way around this?

Student: The problem of habit is grave.

Father: What did your professor say about it?

Student: He said it's grave. But someone in class suggested we send out a colony.

Father: What, to Mars?

Student: Or other places in the galaxy, yes. A place that would begin life-without-rule.

Father: It sounds like a cult.

Student: No it doesn't. Cults are an extreme form of rule.

Father: What about anarchist nudist colonies and the like? Why haven't any of them reached critical mass?

Student: I suspect it's because they're still devoted to the general will.

Director: Remind us. Why is the general will bad?

Student: Because it washes away individuality.

Director: Why is individuality good?

Student: What do you mean?

Director: What's good about being an individual?

Student: You... you... get to be yourself!

Father: Yes, but what is yourself?

Student: When did you become a philosopher?

Father: I was forced to today in listening to you! So, what is yourself?

Student: It's everything you are.

Father: What are you? A soul?

Student: Body and soul. Body and soul in harmony is simply the greatest possible good.

Father: And the general will steals away the soul.

Student: Or part of it, yes.

Father: So this must be the greatest possible bad.

Student: It is.

Father: So whichever government amplifies the general will the most is the worst possible state.

Student: I suppose... that's right.

16

Father: And yet in our democracy part of us does very well.

Student: What do you mean?

Father: The body of 'body and soul'.

Student: You're talking about the benefits of science and technology.

Father: Of course. Only in democracy is this possible.

Director: Science can thrive under other regimes.

Father: What are you saying? The body can do equally well under other regimes?

Student: No, that's nonsense. Democracy serves the body best.

Director: Are you sure it's not our economy that serves the body best?

Father: Do you think our economy is separable from our form of rule?

Director: Many economists seem to think so. Some even suggest better results will follow.

Father: I'm sure they're careful in how they say it.

Director: In varying degrees.

Student: But we have to be careful here not to think an economy can't be a type of rule. We have laws that govern the economy and the economy governs us.

Director: Would you get rid of those laws and let the economy govern us straight?

Student: If it were a natural economy, yes.

Director: Natural in the sense of being without rule.

Student: Yes.

Director: And an unnatural economy is one where corporations rule via chains of command and control.

Student: Or owners rule via their shares.

Father: Would you do away with private property?

Student: I'm not sure.

Father: That's good! Otherwise my money wouldn't be giving you the education that fed this discussion!

Director: Is property the rule over things?

Father: Student, don't tell us you think things have rights.

Student: Property is the rule over others by means of things.

Father: So in your fantasy no one owns anything.

Student: Yes.

Father: How do we live?

Student: I agree that this is hard to see, handicapped as we are by the general will. But I do believe we can.

Director: In communes?

Student: Something like that, I think.

Father: Communes never work. And the ones that do are under unique circumstances.

Student: Life-without-rule is the ultimate unique circumstance.

Father: So what do we do? Barter for everything?

Student: Why not?

Father: We live in a world of extremely complex financial products and dealings. Do you really think we can flip the switch to barter one fine day?

Student: I thought we were going to send out a colony. That colony can operate without the complexities you cite.

Father: But it will be those complexities that pay for the trip! What is that? Original sin?

17

Student: You... make a good point.

Director: Does it help if no one expects the cost of the trip to be repaid?

Student: It does help.

Father: Yes, but the payment will come in the form of knowledge gained. That's what people will hope to get.

Student: We can't give them that.

Father: What do you mean?

Student: I mean, we need to be able to cut the cord. Go dark. Disappear.

Father: Why?

Student: To get rid of the original sin.

Father: That doesn't make any sense. What's wrong with letting others learn?

Student: We have to owe nothing to anyone in order to be a success.

Father: Then no one will fund your trip.

Director: And so there must be an original sin. A lie.

Student: That's right. We're going to lie. We'll promise them what they want, then disappear.

Father: Why do I feel like that's what's happening with the money I give your school?

Student: Dad, don't you know how important this is?

Father: I certainly do. I just look at my accounts and I know exactly how important this is!

Student: But it goes beyond money!

Father: In your fantasy it does. On this planet, under this, the greatest government and society there has ever been, it does not. So finish this course with this crazy professor then see what job you can get talking this way.

Student: Director, tell him.

Director: He's right, Student. You'll need to get a job. In my company they wouldn't take kindly to talk of the abolition of private property. So maybe you have to go dark.

Student: I'll fight effectively from within.

Father: What will you do? Secretly post flyers decrying the injustice of it all?

Student: I would never defend myself with justice.

Father: Why not?

Student: Justice is the ultimate expression of the general will.

Father: Now you're really talking crazy.

Student: There's no need for justice when there's no rule.

Father: So if I come up and steal your chicken, there's no penalty for me?

Student: Why would you steal my chicken?

Father: Because I'm bad.

Student: That's always the sort of argument I hear. It's a gross simplification. People do things for reasons.

Father: Regardless of why they do them, there must be a penalty.

Student: There is a natural penalty. If you're not found out, you suffer from conscience and fears. If you are found out, you lose the respect of your peers.

Father: Or I might just go on living a life of crime.

Student: There is no crime. Only natural consequences for ill considered acts.

18

Father: I'll tell you what the natural consequences of your anarchism will be—you'll never find a job.

Student: Don't tell me. It's because I'm 'not a good fit'—whatever that means.

Director: It generally means you go against the general will.

Father: Yes. You can't walk into an interview and say, 'Hi, I'm an anarchist in the most radical sense.' What will they think? You need to grow out of this phase you're in. Director, can you help me here?

Director: I think the difficulty you point to is real. I think Student's best chance is to find a boss with similar leanings.

Student: How am I supposed to do that?

Director: If you move in anarchist circles, someone might know of a job. And if they know of the job, it might be a good job for you.

Student: What if it pays nothing?

Director: You have to put your money where your mouth is, as they say.

Student: You have a good paying job.

Director: I do.

Student: Was it hard for you to find?

Director: Yes.

Student: How did you find it?

Director: Through a long chain of accidents.

Student: What kind of accidents?

Director: Those involving friends.

Student: Anarchist friends?

Director: No.

Student: But you seem sympathetic to the cause.

Director: I'm sympathetic to you.

Student: So you're saying I need to get my own chain of accidents going with my kind of friends.

Director: Yes, I am.

Student: You're my friend. Can you do anything for me?

Father: Son, I didn't raise you to be so rude.

Director: Oh, it's alright. Student, haven't you thought of talking to your professor? Professors often help good students find jobs.

Student: I guess I didn't think that was a good idea.

Director: Why not?

Student: Because asking for a recommendation or an introduction isn't very... anarchy like.

Director: Why not? You can't recommend or introduce people in a state of anarchy? Or should I say, in life-without-rule?

19

Father: I'm not paying that professor's salary for him not to help you here. Besides, I thought the course was called 'Questioning Democracy', not 'Promoting Anarchy'. Why does anarchy have to follow when you question democracy? Can't you question and find good pro-democracy answers here? I questioned democracy when I was younger. And I concluded that we can do no better.

Student: But that's the thing! I want us to do better!

Director: Father, what good things did you find in democracy?

Father: More people are respected under democratic rule than in any other form of government.

Student: But even more people would be respected in a natural state of anarchy.

Father: Why?

Student: What makes you respect someone?

Father: I respect those who are true to themselves.

Student: Without the general will to get in the way, people are free to be themselves.

Father: But without the challenge of overcoming the general will, what's to be respected? I mean, if we're all free to be ourselves, what's special about being true to yourself? Son, what you describe sounds great. And if I believed anarchy—or life-without-rule, or whatever— were possible, I would be right there with you. But I don't. I think democracy is the best we can do.

Director: Is there a way to make democracy more anarchic?

Father: People often talk about direct democracy—no representatives, direct votes on every important item. To me, that is anarchy—and not in the good sense.

Director: But it's not anarchy-in-the-good-sense because the general will would be given free rein. Am I right, Student?

Student: Yes, that's true.

Director: So if you couldn't have good anarchy, you'd take our system as it is now?

Student: Well, I.... I'm sure... there could be... improvements. But, yes.

Director: What's the biggest problem with our democracy? Is it the effect of the general will?

Student: That is by far the biggest problem.

Director: What can we do about it?

Student: I don't know.

Director: Don't you talk about it in class?

Student: We do. But we get stuck here and can't find an answer.

Director: Is the biggest problem with the general will that it doesn't allow people to be themselves?

Student: It's the conformity effect, yes.

Director: Conformity. But don't people have a million different opinions?

Student: It's more like ten, if we're talking about things of importance.

Director: Why do you think there are only ten, or some similarly small number?

Student: Because of the political process—especially parties.

Director: Would there be millions of opinions in a direct democracy?

Student: Well, people would have to vote—and they'd have to vote for something. 'Should we go to war with Country X? Yes or No.' Two opinions. I think it would be like that for most things.

Father: Yes, but there are counter-examples. Suppose the democracy were voting on healthcare, and there are fifty different proposals to choose from. There would be fifty different opinions. No?

Student: Sure, but when we're talking about hundreds of millions of people, fifty different opinions is shockingly few. The point is that there is a winnowing down of opinion until the general will is reached.

20

Director: What's the real problem with the winnowing process?

Student: Quiet voices aren't heard. Direct democracy is a raucous affair.

Director: What's good about quiet voices?

Student: They speak truth best.

Director: Why?

Student: Quiet voices allow you to think. Loud voices want to force you to believe.

Director: Believe what they're telling you.

Student: Yes, of course.

Director: Is there a sort of violence to loud voices?

Student: There definitely is.

Director: So there's a sort of violence to direct democracy.

Student: Right.

Director: What about the general will? Violent?

Student: In ways we haven't even begun to understand.

Director: And representative democracy?

Student: Violent, too.

Father: Listen to you two. Compared to most other regimes democracy is a gift. How many countries have actual, physical violence on a daily basis? How many have civil war?

Student: We have and have had those things.

Father: Yes, but not to the extent of other places where dictators rule.

Student: I'm not sure about that. The modes may differ, but not the results. Our civil war was one of the worst ever. And we have incredible amounts of gun violence every day.

Father: Yes, but we're free.

Student: Free to obey the general will.

Director: Student, do you think people follow that will without even knowing that's what they're doing?

Student: Sure. They call it being 'normal' and things like that. They think it's just how life is. They're not aware there are other possibilities.

Director: Would you educate them on the possibilities?

Student: Every day. But I want to do it for life-without-rule.

Director: You might be better off starting with little things.

Student: Why?

Director: Because life-without-rule is a big leap. Maybe you can prepare the way for a leap like that by showing people the little things that are viable outside the general will.

Student: I would be training them?

Director: Yes, that's a good way to look at it. You'll help people get comfortable taking small steps.

Student: They'll like the results of their small steps—if they can successfully resist the general will.

Director: That's why we start small. There's less to resist. We have to build up our resistance muscles.

Father: I think that's sensible. But as you resist you might change your mind. Resistance births new thoughts.

Student: I'm open to that.

Father: Good. That's all I can ask. So give us an example of something small that you'd ask people to do.

Student: They should follow your lead. I'd ask them to have tolerance when others speak of life-without-rule.

Director: How many democrats do you think will like to talk about life-without-rule?

Student: Many. Democrats are dreamers at heart. What better dream than this?

21

Director: So what happens if you get a majority dreaming of life-without-rule?

Student: I don't know. But something will happen, that's for sure.

Father: It might cause the democracy to collapse. And then do you know what we'll have? Tyranny.

Student: Maybe. But how do tyrants come to power? They fool the majority. This majority won't be fooled.

Father: Maybe. But then again, what if someone promises them to implement life-without-rule? What if they trust this person? And then what if he or she takes off the sheep's clothes and reveals the wolf?

Student: Well, I admit—that's a problem. The answer is to teach people that implementation of life-without-rule doesn't take a centralized force to do it all at once. It can happen gradually.

Director: Tell us, Student. If ninety percent of the people long for life-without-rule, but ten percent are violently opposed—what happens?

Student: The ninety will do what they can do to bring about as much life-without-rule as they can, and they'll try to persuade the other ten.

Director: What if the ten are the rich and powerful?

Student: Then it might be very hard to persuade them.

Director: Because they see themselves as benefitting from their rule.

Student: Yes. And it's funny you put it that way. We need them to learn that they're not actually benefitting from their rule. To the contrary—they're harmed.

Director: How so?

Student: Rule distorts their souls. Rule requires you to adopt a certain posture. This posture has all sorts of names. Command posture, leadership presence, and so on.

Father: But good leaders love that posture. You're not going to convince them it's bad.

Student: I know. Good leaders are the ultimate problem here. They make bad democracy tolerably good.

Director: So you're hoping for bad leaders?

Student: No. I'm hoping for good leaders—who long for life-without-rule.

Father: But then why would they ever go to the trouble to lead?

Student: They want to lead because they want to make rule smaller and smaller still.

Father: And what, eventually rule just goes away?

Student: It will exist for a very long time. But it will keep on shrinking until its gone.

Father: And if you're wrong?

Student: We'll have good leadership for a while.

22

Father: But what is this effort if not an attempt to replace macro rule with micro rule?

Director: You think rule will never go away.

Father: I do. The desire to rule is in the human soul.

Student: Not every human soul.

Father: I'll grant you that. But all it takes is one wolf to harass the sheep.

Student: But in life-without-rule the people give would-be rulers no point of purchase.

Director: No one will listen to would-be rulers there?

Student: That's right. In order to rule you need one of two things. Opinion that backs you or force. No one who has tried life-without-rule will be of an opinion that leads back to rule. And if everyone is living life-without-rule, who will give the wolf the force it takes to destroy their happy life?

Director: So you're saying once we're there we're there for good.

Student: Correct. It's the getting there that's hard.

Director: And you're in it for the long fight. You don't expect success in your lifetime.

Student: I expect little successes in my lifetime. But the great success? Actual life-without-rule for all? That will take a very long time.

Director: Do you think there will be things about rule that people will miss?

Student: That's another problem. People tend to be fond of things they're used to, even if those things are bad. It has to do with habit and constraint.

Director: What's something they'll miss?

Student: The excitement of elections.

Director: What else?

Student: Having the general will tell you what's normal, what's right.

Director: Comfort and excitement. No small things. Will there be anything like this in life-without-rule?

Student: People will find their own comforts and excitements. And they will be better for the finding.

Father: Will the comfort be as comfortable and the excitement as exciting?

Student: No and yes. These things will be lesser in degree but more satisfying.

Father: Why?

Student: People will need less to satisfy them here.

Director: Does that mean people's appetites will be less in life-without-rule?

Student: It does.

Father: Why?

Student: Humans all have appetites. Rule distorts them, inflates them, brings on fever. Life-without-rule allows the appetites their natural, gentle sway.

Father: So no one will be fat in life-without-rule?

Student: I know you're teasing, but I think it's true. Sure, there will be heavy people for a variety of reasons. But people will be healthier without rule.

Father: What are you going to do about grief?

Student: Excuse me?

Father: Grief. Even though everyone is going to be healthier, people will still die. And there will be those who suffer terrible grief. This can lead to other problems, the ripples of which will spread.

Student: I think grief will be less in life-without-rule.

Father: Why?

Student: Because no one will feel the person didn't live a full and happy life.

Father: What if a child is killed in an accident?

Student: Well, nothing is perfect.

Father: But these accidents might add up and sow the seeds of rule.

Director: How does a child's death lead to rule?

Father: It makes people unhappy. If there is enough unhappiness, people are willing to listen to many sorts of things, some of which might be proposals to reinstate rule.

Director: I think that makes sense. Student?

Student: He has a point. That's why we have to hope for some luck.

Director: Our current democracy was designed not to rely on luck.

Student: Yes, and it's sturdy. But it's only as good as the general will.

23

Director: Can the frame of the democracy be good if the general will is bad?

Student: Something very bad supported by something very good? Yes, that can happen.

Director: When that happens, what's to be done?

Student: We must educate people toward life-without-rule.

Director: And that makes the general will better?

Student: It depends. Are the educated part of the general will? Or do they opt out?

Director: How can they opt out? By not voting?

Student: They don't vote. They don't fulfill any civic duties. They don't let their voice become part of the mass.

Director: So I take it we have your answer. The educated opt out.

Student: Yes, of course they do.

Director: What happens to the general will when sensible people opt out?

Student: It gets worse.

Director: Yet the frame of the democracy supports it nonetheless.

Student: There will come a time when we have to take away the support.

Father: That's dangerous talk.

Student: Oh, we'd do it through legal means.

Father: What, amendments to the frame?

Student: Sure.

Father: Until you've dismantled the whole thing?

Student: Yes.

Father: How long do you think this will take?

Student: Centuries.

Father: Well, that's a relief!

Director: And this process will be taking place across the globe?

Student: Yes, at varying rates. We humans are evolving toward life-without-rule. It's the only way we'll survive.

Father: What about colonies?

Student: We don't have to rely on just one strategy. We're going to need some luck. So let's better our chances.

Father: A world without rule. What happens to ambition?

Student: Ambition to rule? It's gone.

Father: Sure. But what about the ambition to shoot for the stars?

Student: Do you mean discovery? People will be curious. And there will be nothing to stop them following their curiosity—to the stars.

Director: So science will thrive.

Student: Yes, it will play a broader role.

Father: You don't think science is already broad?

Student: Not as broad as it could or should be. In life-without-rule everyone is a sort of scientist. And we'll all contribute freely to the general storehouse of knowledge.

Director: So we're replacing the general will with the general store?

Student: In a general store of knowledge, you can go and take what you want. The general will wants something of you. That's all the difference in the world.

Director: How well does science do in a democracy?

Student: It's limited by the general will.

Father: So all sorts of crazy experiments are possible in life-without-rule?

Student: You only say they're 'crazy' because you're conditioned by the general will. If people don't feel experiments are useful, valid—they won't be performed.

Father: So any crackpot can experiment on whatever he or she likes.

Student: Again, you say 'crackpot' out of conditioning by the general will.

Father: What about immoral experiments?

Student: Cruel experiments on animals, for instance? People wouldn't want to perform them.

Father: I think we're drifting into fantasy land again. I just can't believe you believe people are inherently good.

Student: I'm not saying they're inherently good. I'm saying they're not inherently bad.

24

Director: And the sooner we recognize this fact the better off we'll be?

Student: Yes. Good and bad are functions of rule.

Father: How?

Student: Rulers have to say 'do this' and 'don't do that'. The 'do this' is good; the 'don't do that' is bad. Over the millennia this good-and-bad has built up an unbelievable momentum.

Director: And we fight it through gentle education in life-without-rule.

Student: That's the only way.

Father: So what are we? Followers of Nietzsche? Beyond Good and Evil?

Director: We might also be followers of Rousseau.

Student: What, The Social Contract? We're going exactly against what that says!

Director: As Rousseau went exactly against what others of his day said. That makes us related. No?

Father: Nietzsche, too, said the opposite of what people of his time said. That's part of what philosophers do. But tell me, Director. Do you think my son is a philosopher?

Director: He shows signs. But right now he's more idealist than philosopher.

Student: Philosophers can't be idealists?

Director: We need to ask what an idealist is.

Student: What is an idealist?

Director: Someone who believes in an ideal. Anarchy, in this case.

Student: But why is it an ideal? It's something that could be real.

Director: You've defined idealism. Belief that something unreal could be real.

Student: But for all we know anarchy was the original human state!

Director: For all we know... and we don't know much.

Father: Oh, just own up to it, Son. Anarchy is your ideal against which you judge all things.

Student: So do philosophers hold ideals?

Director: Well, Rousseau taught the General Will. Nietzsche taught the Overman.

Father: The Overman was a rebellion against the General Will. So Student has more in common with Nietzsche than Rousseau.

Student: I have more in common with Chomsky.

Father: Ha! That lunatic?

Student: Why is he a lunatic?

Father: Because he talks about, what is it? Anarcho-syndicalism?

Student: We've been talking about full-bore anarchy and you'd take issue with that?

Father: Full-bore anarchy, as you say, is a dream. I'm happy to while away a pleasant day talking about dreams. But that type of targeted anarchy, the type Chomsky favors, is very real, a real possibility. And it would cause a terribly violent collapse in this country.

Director: You think Chomsky is naive?

Father: That or evil.

Student: How can you say that? He's a very decent man!

Father: Anyone who advocates a position that he or she knows will lead to ruin, is evil. Or don't you agree?

Director: Father, are you suggesting certain people hide behind ideals in order to work harm?

Father: I am.

Director: Why would they do that?

Father: Because they're not strong enough to operate openly.

Student: Why bring ruin?

Father: Because certain people have black hearts. And whether it's by nature or nurture or will, doesn't matter. The fact is that they're black.

Student: Do you think I'm hiding behind an ideal?

Father: Of course not. You're just naive.

25

Director: But his heart might one day turn black?

Father: Yes, there's danger here.

Student: What danger?

Father: One day you might realize you've been naive. This realization might crush your spirit.

Director: What does one do with a crushed spirit?

Father: Some fall into depression. Some want revenge.

Director: Revenge against what?

Father: The world, for not being what you thought it was.

Director: Student, can you see the danger?

Student: I'm fighting the long fight. Even if I suffer defeats, my spirit won't be crushed.

Father: Yes, but you're very young. The young are resilient. Wait until you get older. Defeats sting that much more—because it's not so easy to recover.

Student: So what should I do? Live a lie against what I believe?

Father: No, I'm not saying that. I want you to find your truth. So be careful, Son. Look at everything for what it is, not what you think it should be.

Student: But should is part of is. Potential is inherent to actual. It's the actual that makes the potential what it is.

Father: Then don't be wrong about either.

Student: I don't think I am. And since I'm going to work through gradual education, I'll have time to adjust if I'm wrong.

Father: I like what you're saying.

Director: I do, too. But tell me something, Student. What will people in life-without-rule believe?

Student: Why do you ask that now?

Director: It just occurred to me that we said there'd be some belief in human nature and family. So I wondered if there's more.

Student: More like what?

Director: Democrats believe in democracy. Do anarchists have to believe in anarchy?

Student: Maybe on the way there. But when actually there? They have no need to believe because they're living the fact.

Director: So no belief in anarchy. Must there be belief in anything else in order to sustain this way of life?

Student: I can't see what it would be. Everyone will be free to believe or not believe whatever they like. There's total freedom here.

Director: That sounds very good. I'd like to live in such a state.

Father: Given the chance, what would you believe?

Director: I don't know. It seems to me that we believe based on what we can or can't see. I don't know what view I'd have in life-without-rule. How about you?

Father: I think you make a good point. It's the same for me. Son?

Student: I don't think I'd believe in anything.

Father: What? If you were a scientist, wouldn't you believe you could find the truth?

Student: Well, yes.

Father: That's something you'd believe.

Student: Sure, but I wouldn't believe anything that could get my hopes up too high.

Father: What, are you saying there should be no hope in life-without-rule?

Student: It sounds bad to say we shouldn't have too much hope. But we have to ask why people do.

Father: They're not happy where they are. Or they believe they could be happier still.

Student: Well, people will be happy in life-without-rule. And they will be content.

Father: This sounds like Nietzsche's Last Man.

Student: What's wrong with that?

Father: These people will do nothing great!

Student: And?

Father: You're making my point. Don't you feel a longing for the great?

Student: Life-without-rule will be great, the greatest thing ever.

Father: Yes, but what happens as time passes? Won't people grow restless?

Student: Are the happy ever restless?

Father: Maybe they don't know they're happy.

Student: I don't see how that's possible.

Father: Wait until you get older and you might see.

Student: Maybe. I'm open to that. But what has the great brought us other than wars and other ills?

Father: Are you forgetting about art?

Student: There will be plenty of great art in life-without-rule.

Father: Somehow I doubt it.

Student: Why?

Father: Great art is born of suffering.

Student: Not necessarily.

Father: We can agree to disagree.

Student: I'll say this. If you're right, great art only comes after the artist finds a way out.

Father: And if I'm right, and life-without-rule is all you think it will be, I think you're going to have, at best—folk art.

Student: What's wrong with folk art?

Father: Nothing—but it's not great.

Student: You must never have been to a folk dance.

Father: You might be surprised what I've been to. Yes, a folk dance can be great. But it's no Telemann.

Student: Troubled souls need someone like a Telemann to sooth them. We won't have troubled souls.

Father: I honestly wish that were true.

Student: Make the experiment. Teach the benefits of life-without-rule. In the process you might convince yourself.

Father: That's a unique approach—teaching others in order to persuade yourself.

Student: It happens all the time. Teachers start out believing, grow discouraged, but learn from their students and are refreshed.

Father: And how do you know this?

Student: My professor tells us this all the time. But you know what? I think great art can refresh those of us in life-without-rule.

Director: Why would you need refreshing?

Student: We all, no matter how happy we are, grow tired at times, frustrated at times. Great art can give us a lift. And we can learn from that great art in order to make more great art. So it's not just folk music for us. To think so is to reduce the human spirit to something less than it is.

Director: But what of suffering?

Student: Suffering isn't eradicated. After all, we can fall and break our leg. There's suffering there. People can seize on what they know of suffering and apply their imagination. They can see what great suffering must be like. And they can create art from that perspective.

Father: It's one thing to imagine. It's another to live.

Student: But some of us can imagine the heights of suffering.

Father: But to create we have to live this suffering.

Student: How do you know?

Father: I just know.

Student: That's like saying I know life-without-rule existed in the pre-history of man. I don't. I believe what I believe; you believe what you believe. That's all we can say.

27

Director: Well, I hope we get the opportunity to see what artists in life-without-rule can do.

Father: So you'd take creature happiness over sublime art?

Director: I'd take both.

Father: But if you had to choose?

Director: Would you choose the sublime over happiness?

Student: Sublimity stems from the longing to break with the general will.

Father: Of course that's what you think.

Student: What do you think suffering is?

Father: What do you mean?

Student: Suffering happens when you go against the general will.

Father: Suffering happens when you break your leg.

Student: Yes, but that's not the kind of suffering you care about.

Father: Care about?

Student: You, at heart, don't want to lose your suffering.

Father: That's ridiculous.

Student: Is it? I think you suffer because you're willing to go against the general will. And you're proud of the fact. You don't want to lose your pride. You are defined by your pride. And it's a sublime and noble pride. You love great art because it speaks to your pride. If great art goes away, nothing speaks to your pride. And so you fear life-without-rule because it might take away your art. It might isolate your pride. It might take your pride away.

Director: Is there pride in life-without-rule?

Student: There's self-love. But is there pride? No.

Director: Then I'd say your father is right to fear life-without-rule.

Student: But we haven't said what we mean by pride.

Director: What do we mean by pride?

Student: An overbearing assertion of your idea of your worth.

Director: Is an appropriate assertion of your idea of your worth okay?

Student: Of course. That's what I mean by self-love. People feel worth in life-without-rule. They love themselves for this. But they aren't aggressive about it. Don't you think that's healthy?

Director: I do. But now that we speak of health, there's something I wonder. Which is healthier, a simple life or a life that has so much more?

Student: Oh, a simple life of course. That's what those in life-without-rule will have. Simple needs, simple pleasures, simple love for oneself and others.

Director: So you would side with Socrates over Glaucon.

Student: I don't know what you mean.

Director: In the Republic, Socrates speaks with young Glaucon, Plato's brother. Glaucon hungers for more than a simple way of life, more than a simple life like your life-without-rule can provide.

Father: Hold on. Are you comparing me to Glaucon?

Director: Well, you wouldn't be Socrates. Socrates says he would be happy with a simple life, a life before the city becomes feverish with desires. And it's funny—

Father: Yes, but sublime and feverish are different things.

Student: No, I think Director has a point. But why is it funny?

Director: Because no one pays any attention to what Socrates says about what would make him content. So he goes on and elaborates the city of philosophers that everyone remembers.

Student: You think people will pay no attention to me.

Director: You'll have to tell me what your experience is as time goes on.

Father: No one will listen. For sure. Plato knew this. The young will ruin it all.

Student: How so?

Father: They won't appreciate what you're offering them.

Student: But they will learn.

Father: Not before they make what will amount to terrible mistakes.

Student: Is it any better in a democracy?

Father: No, I'm not saying that. But democracies like ours are made to withstand a great many shocks. Not so your life-without-rule. There is nothing there to sustain any sort of tremor.

Student: But our youths won't shock our way of life.

Father: You're not old enough to see how things work. But tell me why you think they won't shock.

Student: Our youths won't be corrupt. Glaucon was corrupted by corrupt Athenian democracy.

Director: Why wasn't Socrates corrupted?

Student: Maybe he was. But he overcame it—with philosophy.

Director: What's the worst sort of political and moral corruption?

Student: That of a degenerate kingship.

Father: That's what Rousseau lived through.

Student: And he overcame it with philosophy.

Director: How do you know he overcame?

Student: He taught the General Will in the face of absolute monarchy.

Director: So what should we teach in the face of absolute democracy?

Student: We don't have absolute democracy.

Director: If we did?

Father: Then we would teach what Nietzsche taught.

Director: But if we taught what's appropriate to what we have now?

Student: We'd teach life-without-rule.

Father: I thought we'd teach life-without-rule no matter what.

Student: Well, yes, we would.

Father: So Nietzsche was wrong? Rousseau was wrong? Was any philosopher ever right?

Student: I don't claim to be an expert on the history of philosophy. But I'd say Chomsky is close to right.

Director: Because he's from our time?

Student: Probably, yes.

Director: Was Rousseau closest to right for his time?

Student: Maybe.

Director: And Nietzsche?

Student: I don't know. Nietzsche was a marginal figure in his time. Rousseau was one of the most famous men of his age.

Director: Why does that matter?

Student: I guess it doesn't.

Director: Fame has nothing to do with quality of thought?

Student: No, it doesn't.

Director: Will people desire to be famous in life-without-rule?

Student: Maybe.

Director: Why?

Father: Because they want to overcome death.

Director: I thought there would be no fear of death in life-without-rule.

Student: You can want to be immortal without fearing death.

Director: And fame brings immortality.

Student: As much of it as we're allowed.

Director: Can longing for immortality bring great art?

Student: Yes.

Director: And is that because longing for immortality brings suffering?

Student: I... don't know.

Father: All longing brings suffering.

Director: Or maybe all suffering brings longing.

Student: Either way, there is neither in life-without-rule.

Father: So people just sort of casually want immortality?

Student: Now I'm not sure if they even want fame.

Director: Tell me something, Student. Is love immortal?

Student: True love is, yes, of course.

Director: And by true you mean requited?

Student: I do.

Director: Will all love be requited in life-without-rule?

Student: Even I don't believe that.

Director: So there will be suffering?

Student: Yes. But it will be less devastating than in life-under-rule.

Father: Why?

Student: Love will be gentler than it is now.

Director: All love?

Student: Yes.

29

Director: How is love in democracy?

Student: The same as it is in any sort of rule.

Director: What does that mean?

Student: All love fights against the general will.

Director: Why?

Student: Because love is emphatically non-general. It's specific, particular.

Director: So love has its hardest fight when the general is strongest—which is in a democracy?

Student: I haven't thought this through. Love under rule always has a fight. But maybe it is harder in a democracy.

Director: Hmm.

Student: What's wrong?

Director: All sorts of love flourish in democracy. No?

Father: Of course! Love is more free here than anywhere else.

Student: Maybe.

Director: Is it better in life-without-rule?

Student: No doubt. There, love can be love without a fight.

Father: You're not very experienced in love.

Student: No one in democracy can have the full experience of love as long as the general will is intact.

Father: Why not?

Student: The general will clouds who we are. We can't reciprocate love fully without knowing each other for just what we are.

Director: Can democrats hope for a break in the cloudy sky of general will?

Student: Maybe now and then, I suppose. A lucky break. But in general? No. Democracy emphatically gives voice to the general will. That's what it does.

Director: Can we change what it does?

Student: Not as long as people believe that's what it should do.

Director: Let's say they don't believe. What then?

Father: Hold on. What are we talking about? Democracy does what it does without our belief? Are we saying we just go through the motions and vote?

Director: Yes. What then?

Student: Every minority in an important vote will be disenchanted.

Director: What's the effect of that?

Father: Trouble.

Director: Why?

Father: Because then they'll be susceptible to beliefs like life-without-rule.

Director: Each minority will defect, so to speak?

Student: They'll come to believe in life-without-rule.

Father: More likely they'll come to believe in some other form of rule.

Director: Until there are hardly any left who believe in democracy?

Father: Yes.

Student: That's why it's so important we educate toward life-without-rule.

Father: Oh, I thought the notion of free love would draw them there on its own.

Student: Please don't mock. It won't be a life of license, Dad.

Father: Why not?

Student: Because libertines are born of repression.

Director: What of those born of democracy and its general will?

Student: They have no need for licentious acts once they're free. They'll feel relief.

Father: Free of excessive desire?

Student: Yes, exactly—free of the tyranny in their souls.

Father: Tyranny?

Director: Student, look at you blush! Are you embarrassed?

Student: All of us who have thought great thoughts have known the tyranny in the soul.

Director: What are great thoughts?

Student: Thoughts that overcome the general will.

Director: And if there is no general will to overcome?

Student: I suppose there will be no great thoughts.

Director: Can people be happy with no great thoughts?

Student: Yes. There's no need for those thoughts.

Father: But don't you think that something is lost?

Student: Let it be lost.

Director: You wouldn't want to preserve these thoughts in history lessons and the like?

Student: No, let them be lost. They will have served their purpose. Better to have people happy—without the shadows these thoughts must bring.

Father: You'll pull the ladder up after you—as your colony would.

Student: Yes.

Director: You won't even take credit for your own grand thoughts?

Student: Why would I? The prize of life-without-rule is so great I'd need nothing else.

Father: That's selfless of you.

Student: No, it's selfish. I want the greater prize.

Director: Some would choose fame over that prize.

Student: That's because they're overcome by the general will. They want to be generally known.

Director: People won't want to be known in life-without-rule?

Student: Of course they will. And they'll be known by those who are close. To want more than that is folly.

Director: Why?

Student: Because we can't be known from a distance.

Father: We can't know Rousseau or Nietzsche? We can only know Chomsky because he's of our age?

Student: It's very hard to know others from another age. But even with Chomsky, few are close.

Director: Is that because he's a philosopher?

Student: No, it's because he's a human being.

Father: Well, humans are hard to know even when right in front of our face.

Director: Will it be any easier to know them in life-without-rule?

Student: Yes, it will.

Director: Why?

Student: Because our selves get twisted and caught up in the general will. And so they're hard to recognize for what they are.

Director: What are they? All the same?

Father: This is where Nietzsche's Last Man comes in.

Student: No. They're not all the same. They have important things in common. But they differ nonetheless.

Director: How do they differ?

Student: They just... differ!

Director: They have different bodies?

Student: No, you can't reduce it to that.

Director: Why not?

Student: Because that's... shallow!

Director: Their souls differ?

Student: Yes.

Director: What makes up the soul?

Student: What do you mean? Souls... are souls!

Father: I remember what I learned in philosophy class. The regime shapes the soul. There are aristocratic souls, kingly souls, and democratic souls—as well as the opposites of those regimes.

Student: What philosopher taught that?

Father: Plato.

Director: So if there's no regime, is there no soul?

Student: That's impossible. We all have souls. More so in life-without-rule.

Director: Why?

Student: The will of the regime tramples upon our souls. Without that will, our souls are free to be what they are.

Director: What are they?

Father: Unique like snowflakes. Ha, ha.

Student: Why do you laugh at what's true?

Father: I laugh because in life-without-rule what difference is there between souls? Isn't life-without-rule the most shallow sort of life? Everything is on the surface there. What's wrong?

Student: I never... thought about that.

Father: Oh, don't be upset. Just don't be surprised when that's what you get.

31

Director: What's wrong with everything being on the surface?

Student: I guess there's nothing... wrong.

Director: But you're wondering what's right?

Student: Yes. And I'm wondering what happens to philosophy.

Director: How so?

Student: Philosophy seeks to get under the surface of things.

Director: Why would it do that?

Student: Because it wants to get at the truth.

Director: Won't it still want truth if truth is on the surface?

Student: Sure, but then there's nothing special about philosophy.

Director: What's wrong with that?

Student: You don't want to be special?

Director: I thought we were all special in life-without-rule.

Student: Yes, but....

Director: I think I understand part of your concern. It has to do with philosophy's love of wisdom. What wisdom is there in life-without-rule?

Student: All the old will be wise.

Director: Why?

Student: Because of their experience.

Director: Will the young listen to the old?

Student: Most of them will.

Director: Who will check to see if the old are truly wise and worth listening to?

Student: Philosophers.

Director: Philosophers are the guardians here?

Student: Yes. But why do you think the old might not be wise?

Director: Maybe they're senile.

Student: But everyone will know if that's the case.

Director: There are varying degrees of senility. Philosophers can spot it right away.

Student: Then philosophers have some use. But why can't everyone tell? And how does someone become a philosopher?

Director: You're asking a hard question. I speak of one question because, at heart, your two questions are the same. In life-without-rule people will be trusting, I think. And the young will trust the old. Philosophers are less trusting. So how would they arise?

Student: They have experience that makes them less trusting.

Director: How? Isn't everyone's experience good in life-without-rule?

Student: Yes, but there will be accidents.

Director: Philosophers arise by accident? That has the spark of truth. What kind of accident?

Student: Who can say? How did you become a philosopher?

Father: Yes, Director. How?

Director: My questions led me to this. But how did I have my questions? I don't know. They were always there, as far back as I can remember.

Father: Well, we can speculate on this no end. The fact is you had questions. The question I have is—what if no one has questions in life-without-rule?

Student: Anyone who is alive has questions.

Father: Even if everything is perfect? What questions would they have?

Student: We're not saying everything is perfect. We're saying we're free from interference from the general will.

32

Director: Are we certain there's no way for democracy to exist without the general will?

Student: We are.

Father: But there were democracies long before Rousseau.

Student: He only gave voice to what had existed in the past.

Director: I'm not so sure about that.

Student: Do you think he created modern democracy?

Director: No. I think he may, however, have educated people toward that sort of rule.

Student: Sort of like what I will do for life-without-rule?

Director: Yes.

Student: You really think I can be like Rousseau?

Father: Why be like him? Rousseau was troubled, Son.

Student: By those around him, yes.

Father: He went crazy in the end.

Student: That may be. But that doesn't mean he didn't do great things.

Father: Look who's talking! You, who would undermine the general will, stand in defense of Rousseau?

Student: Democracy points to life-without-rule. Rousseau took us one step closer.

Father: But the general will, the greatest obstacle to life-without-rule, is strongest in democracy!

Student: So much better for us to see it for what it is. It's darkest before the dawn.

Director: I think there's truth in that. But why not side with Nietzsche?

Student: What, and be a crazed mountain man like his Zarathustra? No.

Director: Do you think it's inevitable we'll come to life-without-rule?

Student: As I said, not inevitable—no. But more and more likely as the education spreads.

Director: You'll teach one, and they'll teach another—and so on, and so on?

Student: Yes. But I'll teach two, and they'll teach two more—and so on, and so on.

Director: And it will work because they'll all remember that moment of freedom after birth.

Student: That's right. We'll bring it home.

Director: Does democracy ever feel like home?

Student: No, democracy feels like constant agitation.

Director: And people don't want agitation.

Student: No. People want peace. Life-without-rule can bring them that.

Father: Will people be bored?

Student: No! There's so much good in life lived well that it's never boring, not for a moment.

Father: That promise will win many to your cause. I hope you're right.

Director: Why does boredom exist today?

Student: The general will causes us to shy away from what we'd truly like to do. So we watch popular shows, and so on, just to kill time.

Director: Why doesn't the general will say for us to live our true lives?

Student: It's because of the winnowing. We all start out that way, wanting to live our true lives. But as our personal desires combine with those of countless others, an awful sort of compromise is reached, one that offends few and satisfies none.

Director: He has a point, Father, don't you think?

Father: He does. But we can invest in countering the general will while recogniz-ing that this will keeps the peace and makes many great things possible.

Student: Hypocrisy?

Father: Realism.

Student: I think democracy demands of us many false priests.

Father: What do you mean?

Student: Supporters of the regime who don't believe what they preach.

Father: You think I'm such a priest?

Student: Haven't you just said?

Director: I think your father is talking about the general will as a necessary evil.

Student: Does that make it any better?

Father: You don't think it's good to preach the necessary?

Student: I don't think it's necessary.

Director: Why not?

Student: Because people know full well what's necessary in their lives. They don't need anyone to preach.

33

Director: I'm going to ask one more time, just to be sure. There's no democracy without the general will?

Student: Tell me what it would be like.

Director: People vote. But they don't let the outcome shape who they are.

Father: That sounds sensible.

Student: I don't see how it's possible. Unless the votes are meaningless, they will shape people's lives to a certain degree.

Father: A certain degree, sure. But that means to a certain degree they won't.

Director: Your father has a point.

Student: What, are you arguing in favor of democracy now?

Director: If you can get people away from the general will to a certain degree, isn't that a step toward what you want?

Student: I suppose.

Director: People can be strong. Educate them to take this step. You might be doing the greatest service that can be done.

Student: But isn't a democracy without the general will... hollow?

Director: Why would it be? Who says you have to believe in your regime? Isn't it enough to live by its rules and thrive?

Father: He has a point.

Student: But isn't it morally bankrupt to live but not believe?

Director: Why would it be?

Student: Because.... I don't know.

Director: Exactly. You don't know. Try it and see. After all, are you going to stop living by the rules of our democracy because you see a better way?

Student: No, I'm going to live by those rules while I educate toward the better way.

Director: Are you morally bankrupt?

Student: Of course not!

Director: Then how can you blame others?

Father: He has a very good point. I'm one of those others. Please don't blame me.

Student: I won't. But isn't this to advocate a democracy without soul?

Father: People have souls. Not regimes. And, despite Plato, I don't believe the regime makes up our soul.

Student: Well, I don't believe that either. How can I? I'm a born democrat. Do I have an inherently democratic soul?

Father: No, you don't—as you've shown amply today.

Director: What's a democratic soul like?

Father: It believes in freedom.

Student: I believe in freedom.

Father: It's mistrustful of authority.

Student: I'm mistrustful of authority.

Father: It believes in the wisdom of the crowd.

Student: That's where I differ.

Director: Where do you get your wisdom?

Student: Truth be told? I don't get much.

Director: Where would you get wisdom in life-without-rule?

Student: Maybe I wouldn't. And that might be okay.

Director: Why do we need wisdom here, in democracy?

Student: Here wisdom, real wisdom, serves the purpose of countering the general will.

Director: And fake wisdom?

Student: It's just the general will in disguise.

34

Father: You really don't think the people know best?

Student: You really don't think the people know best.

Father: True.

Director: Can they ever come to know best?

Student: If we educate them toward life-without-rule, sure.

Director: And that's all it takes? Education?

Student: Well, it does take something more.

Father: Now you worry me, Son.

Director: What more is there?

Student: Taking steps whenever you can.

Father: Steps? You'd undermine rule?

Student: Yes.

Father: You can't!

Student: Why not?

Father: Why not! Haven't you heard of treason? Or has your professor conveniently forgotten to talk about that?

Student: Oh, I'm not talking about things like that.

Director: What are you talking about?

Student: For instance? If I'm a manager, I wouldn't rule my employees. I'd introduce them to life-without-rule.

Father: And your boss would introduce you to the door!

Student: That's the chance I'd take.

Father: Very easy to say when you're young and in school.

Director: How else might you implement life-without-rule?

Student: One day if I'm a father, I wouldn't rule my son.

Father: You have no idea what kind of trouble that brings.

Student: If it does, it's because of the general will.

Father: It doesn't matter why it happens; it matters that it does! Think about it. Wouldn't you want to educate your son about the general will?

Student: Of course.

Father: What do you think such education is if it's not rule?

Student: Education isn't rule.

Father: Oh yes it is. Director?

Director: I think your father has a point.

Student: But there's education and then there's education.

Director: What's the bad kind?

Student: The kind that tells you what to think.

Director: And the good kind?

Student: The kind that shows you how to think.

35

Director: What's there to think about in life-without-rule?

Student: What do you mean? There will be plenty to think about! What's there to think about now?

Director: How to escape from the general will.

Student: And once the escape is made, that's it?

Director: That's what I'm asking you.

Student: Of course that's not it. We think about more than escape today.

Director: What do we think about?

Student: Life, love, the future, the past. You know.

Director: Maybe in life-without-rule we'll think about, for instance, how best to grow our food—as well as about life, love, the future, the past?

Student: Yes, of course. We'll think about all sorts of things concerning how we sustain and live our lives.

Director: But will anything keep us as sharp as trying to escape the general will?

Student: Are you suggesting we might lose our fighting form?

Director: I'm not suggesting. I'm asking. Will we? What will be our fight?

Student: We don't need a fight to stay sharp.

Director: Will we play-fight for exercise?

Student: Sure.

Director: What will we play-fight about?

Student: Oh, I don't know. Anything.

Director: Maybe we can play-fight about whether we need to fight.

Student: What, like a debate?

Director: Sure, debates might be good. They might be fun.

Father: Provided people don't lust to win.

Director: Who takes fun seriously?

Student: No one will in life-without-rule.

Director: Why not? Is it the general will that makes people serious about fun?

Student: It is.

Director: How?

Student: It wants us to compete.

Director: Why?

Student: Competition raises the bar.

Director: What bar?

Student: The bar that tells us if we measure up to the standard of the general will.

Director: And let me guess. We can never measure up.

Student: Never.

Director: So everyone strives to measure up and fails.

Student: Precisely.

Director: And this failure hurts so much we can't even have any fun?

Student: That's how it goes. We feel such an urgent need to win, to measure up, to be a winner—we trample harmless fun.

36

Father: But not everyone measures themselves against the general will.

Student: True. A handful measure themselves against a different standard.

Director: And the rest?

Student: They reference the general will. It shapes what they think and believe.

Director: What will shape them in life-without-rule?

Student: Their own life. Their experiences, decisions, loves—everything but some general will.

Director: But won't a sort of general will appear on its own?

Student: What do you mean?

Director: Won't there be popular thought? Won't it be expressed in books, shows, news, and so on?

Student: Yes, but it won't be considered the source of wisdom. It won't be the source of law.

Director: Okay. But the things that do shape them, their choices for instance— will they always be good?

Student: Yes.

Father: Ha!

Student: You laugh, but without the general will to interfere the right choices will always be clear.

Director: And if clear they'll be made.

Student: Of course.

Director: So there will no mistakes?

Student: Not that kind of mistake.

Director: Is it sort of like it is with animals?

Student: I'm not following.

Director: I mean, do we ever see animals making these kinds of mistakes?

Student: No, we don't.

Director: Animals know what they are and live what they are.

Student: Yes.

Director: Even when they live in herds.

Student: If they're herd animals, yes.

Director: Are humans herd animals?

Student: No.

Director: So we won't find humans living like sheep in life-without-rule.

Student: We won't.

Director: But we find humans living like sheep in democracies?

Student: Sometimes we do.

Director: And that's against their nature.

Student: Right. And it's due to the power of the general will.

37

Director: Are people afraid of the general will?

Student: Very much so.

Director: Why?

Student: Because it's a tremendous force beyond their control.

Director: And yet it comes from them.

Student: That's the irony here.

Director: This force, it's what winnows our choices?

Student: Yes, and we might also say the winnowing increases the force.

Father: Would the general will have less force if we could choose from a million candidates?

Student: For half a million offices?

Father: No, for one office.

Student: Could a plurality win? Or would it take a simple majority?

Father: A plurality.

Student: That would leave a lot of dissatisfied people.

Director: How does that affect the general will?

Student: It might make it worse.

Director: Even if dissatisfaction drives many into the arms of anarchy?

Student: Well...

Father: It would drive them toward direct democracy first.

Director: Would direct democracy face the same problem if there's no winnowing on an issue and a plurality can win?

Student: It would.

Director: Is the answer to require a simple majority?

Student: No, because you'd never arrive at that without a massive winnowing.

Director: How does life-without-rule handle these sorts of things?

Student: There consensus forms without the need for a vote.

Director: How is that possible?

Student: Everyone has a voice, one that that isn't melted down into general will. The voice of the people in life-without-rule is rich and complex—and we never stop the dialogue. We are always adjusting, never stuck.

Father: It sounds a lot like a general will to me.

Student: The general will culminates in law, the ultimate tool of rule. We have none of that. And so we're more alive.

38

Father: That's a big claim. But how else does life-without-rule differ from the general will?

Student: The general will uses a megaphone when it speaks. We in life-without-rule use a natural voice, one that carries as far as it carries and no more.

Director: What's the problem with the megaphone?

Student: It frightens the gentler souls.

Director: How do the gentle fare in life-without-rule?

Student: They positively thrive.

Director: What would happen if someone were to produce a megaphone and shout in life-without-rule?

Student: That person would be shunned.

Director: And shunning is a serious penalty.

Student: Of course.

Director: Might this person not want revenge for being shunned?

Student: I don't think so. There would be no hard feelings. The person would absorb the lesson and move on.

Father: I think we're in fantasy land again.

Student: But it all makes sense. People are sensitive to slights, yes. But as soon as the megaphone stops, the shunning would, too. Sure, there might be some good natured teasing of the loud one. But that's about it. Why should there be more? The person stops as soon as—

Father: —the general will is known.

Student: No, it's no general will.

Father: What is it?

Student: Individual preferences for no loud voice.

Director: Why don't those preferences add up to a general will?

Student: Because they're never enacted into law! There's no hope that they would ever be enacted into law. The general will and law go hand in hand—even when not enacted into law. The hope of it becoming law is everything here.

Director: Why?

Student: Because people then will advocate and agitate for a vote.

Director: There is no agitation in life-without-rule?

Student: None. There is, of course, persuasion. But no agitation.

Father: There's nothing unpleasant in life-without-rule.

Student: I'm not saying that.

Father: Sure you are. Everything will be just fine if we take away rule. But let me hear you out. What unpleasantness is there in life-without-rule?

Student: Well, people still have to work.

Father: I thought you'd say that without the general will, people will know what work suits them best, and they will find happiness and satisfaction in it.

Student: You do have a point.

Father: Ha! What other unpleasantness will there be?

Student: Loved ones will grow sick or old and die.

Father: What else?

Student: That's all I can think of right now.

39

Director: Father, what's the harm in giving this a try?

Father: Are you serious? Who would agree to go along?

Director: If we go the route of a colony, I think we'd have sufficient volunteers.

Father: There are enough crazy people in the world, sure. But how do you get around this problem? The people we'd send to the colony, their personalities will have been shaped by the general will.

Director: Then we have to send them as young as we can, because they'll still be pliable and can learn, grow, and reshape themselves over time.

Father: How old?

Director: No older than Student, here.

Student: I wish we had the technology to make the trip.

Director: And then the money, yes.

Student: I wish you could come, too.

Director: My work is here, challenging the general will.

Student: Your challenge might only make it stronger.

Director: How?

Student: You point out its weak spots and then it adjusts.

Director: That's why I challenge its strengths, my friend.

Student: Come with us to the colony. While we're establishing ourselves, you can help ensure no general will takes root.

Director: And after you're established, what would I do?

Student: Live!

Director: As a philosopher? Philosophers question people's beliefs. Will the colonists have beliefs?

Student: Of course they will.

Director: Then I'll have work to do.

Student: You want to question us so we hold only the best possible beliefs. I think that's right, and good.

Father: I don't think these young anarchists are going to have many beliefs out there.

Director: When beliefs are few they're usually strong. It may take a lifetime to persuade them to see things for what they are.

Student: Why do you assume we'll be blinded by our beliefs?

Father: Live as long as we have and you might understand.

40

Student: What, are you going to argue in favor of a gerontocracy?

Father: Rule of the old? I bet that's a milder rule than that of the young. Director?

Director: I think it depends on many factors.

Father: Yes, but let's try it out in our democracy. We'll just raise the voting age to fifty, or sixty-five. I bet fewer rash decisions would be made.

Student: Fewer bold steps would be taken.

Director: What's the difference between bold and rash?

Student: Rash is ill advised. Bold takes courage.

Director: Maybe the elders will ask the youths to perform bold acts.

Father: In my experience, youth is willing.

Director: What makes them willing?

Father: Mainly? They trust their elders.

Director: Student, is intergenerational trust possible in life-without-rule?

Student: Of course. In fact, it's more likely here.

Director: Why?

Student: What do we trust in people?

Director: Their truth.

Student: Yes! In life-without-rule, people's truth is unclouded by general will.

Director: So it's easier to have well-placed trust in life-without-rule.

Student: It is.

Father: Is there anything that's not better in life-without-rule?

Student: No.

Father: Director, I'm worried my son has blind faith.

Director: His faith depends on a great deal of luck. There are so many things that can go wrong and upset the balance of life-without-rule.

Student: I know it depends on luck, especially to get started. But if we can gain some momentum? I think life-without-rule can last.

Director: Do you believe there can be varying degrees of life-without-rule, or is it an all-or-nothing affair?

Student: For it to work it has to be an all-or-nothing affair.

Father: That answer doesn't allay my fears.

Director: Student, I thought you were going educate toward life-without-rule.

Student: I am. But a time comes when we have to make the leap. That's why I think a colony would be great. We'll make a literal leap into space.

Father: But even if you go dark—and maybe especially if you go dark—people will follow in your steps, people not committed to life-without-rule.

Student: We won't admit them to the colony.

Director: So what do you have? A test to see how anarchic a person is? And what if people sincerely wish to join you, but when they do they find themselves pining for rule?

Student: That won't happen. Life-without-rule is so much better than life-under-rule.

Director: To know it is to love it?

Student: Yes.

Director: Because it awakens that sense of freedom we once knew.

Student: Exactly. Nothing is finer in the world.

Director: Not even love?

Father: That will be your biggest source of trouble.

Student: Why? What's wrong with love?

Father: Maybe nothing with love itself; but everything with love unrequited.

Student: Jealousy?

Father: Of course! A terrible, very real force. Or do you think it's just a problem of the general will?

41

Student: It's a problem of the general will.

Father: Ha!

Director: How so, Student?

Student: When our feelings are pure, we only love those who love us back. It's the ultimate in natural selection.

Director: So if no one loves us back, we don't love?

Student: We don't. We devote ourselves to other things.

Father: Naive.

Student: I'm only following human nature.

Father: There's nothing natural in your natural state of life-without-rule!

Student: You're mistaking millenniums-old customs for nature—customs based on varying degrees of general will.

Father: And what are you basing your view on? Hope?

Student: Yes.

Director: That's quite a confession.

Student: I'm willing to give this a try. I'm willing to live up to my hope.

Father: Well, as long as you're not talking about violent revolution, I suppose that's admirable, if crazy, Son.

Student: Thanks, I think.

Father: So what will you do? Seek to sway the general will to take up the cause of life-without-rule?

Student: What, tell it to dismantle itself?

Father: It can sacrifice itself for the greater good. Director?

Director: He can ask people to exchange their Voice for a voice.

Father: Yes, but the Voice makes them strong.

Student: But it's an illusion. There's real power in a firm individual voice, not some general Voice.

Father: But people feel safety in numbers.

Director: Is life-without-rule a life of risk?

Student: It is. Real risk. But that's what's so attractive here. Everything is at stake. Our choices matter because they have direct effect. This gives life zest.

Father: At least now you're talking some sense. But can you live with the danger?

Student: Yes. Life-without-rule takes us back to our original state, to freedom—to life. And there's danger here.

42

Director: And if danger, fear?

Father: What, no answer, Son? Is there really fear in perfect life-without-rule?

Student: I never said things will be perfect.

Father: How could they be? Just take the most basic fear—the fear of death. That's a universal fear.

Director: But why fear death if you're living a happy life?

Father: You don't want that life to end!

Student: But if you get old enough, you do want your life to end. And youth is too caught up in itself to worry much about death.

Father: Are you seriously saying there will be no fear of death?

Student: Not an overwhelming fear. Maybe a little fear, on the side.

Director: So what's the serious fear? What's the danger in life?

Student: That life-without-rule will end.

Director: Rule is the fear.

Student: Yes. Unless life-without-rule is global, there will be outside forces of concern.

Director: There will be wars, you mean.

Student: Yes, there will be wars.

Father: Why? Will the anarchists start them?

Student: No. Other powers will covet what we have.

Father: Or they'll think you're evil.

Student: Whatever the reason, these powers won't let us be. And so we'll have to fight. And the necessity to fight causes fear, even among the brave.

Director: But if life-without-rule were global? What is there to fear?

Student: There probably is no fear.

Father: I thought fear was part of life.

Student: Maybe I'm wrong. Would that be so bad?

Director: Few who fear would say losing their fear is bad. What's the fear in democracy?

Student: Empire-democracy fears letting go of the tiger's tail.

Director: You mean everyone will turn on them if given the chance.

Student: Yes.

Director: What else do they fear?

Student: Going against the general will. And that's an all-pervasive fear.

Director: Fear without, fear within. You'd think they'd give anarchy a chance.

Student: Life-without-rule involves letting go of the tail.

Director: So there can be no transition from empire-democracy to life-without-rule?

Student: I guess I never thought this through. I think that's right. Democracy can never let go of the tail.

Director: So a colony is the only real choice?

Student: If an empire is at stake? Yes.

43

Director: So why bother to educate toward life-without-rule in an empire?

Student: There probably isn't a point, en masse. But there is a point in educating potential colonists.

Director: How will you recognize their potential?

Student: They'll have a certain openness to things. And they'll long for peace.

Father: They'll be pacifists?

Student: They'll be willing to fight for our life-without-rule. But they'll be fighting for peace.

Director: Life-without-rule brings peace.

Student: Yes.

Director: Will there be inter-personal fights?

Student: No.

Father: Ha! Again with the perfect world. What if someone drifts from the faith, so to speak?

Student: You mean they want to rule?

Father: Rule, sure. Won't there be a fight then?

Student: I suppose in an imperfect anarchy....

Director: Won't all anarchies start out imperfectly? Or can one come into existence fully formed?

Student: Well, even in a colony old habits will be hard to break.

Director: So even there there might be attempts, however minor, at rule.

Student: True.

Director: In a colony, where would you send the would-be ruler? Back home?

Student: If possible, yes.

Father: And if he or she gathers forces to return and take control of the anarchy?

Student: Why would they do that? What has the anarchy got? We'll be living in a colony on some forsaken planet. No riches. Nothing to exploit.

Father: Yes, but you'll have—pride.

44

Director: Pride is an affront?

Father: To those who lack it, yes.

Director: Who has pride in a democracy?

Father: Those who resist the general will. Son, are you surprised?

Student: No. I know you resist the general will to some extent. And you have pride.

Director: Are you still interested in making the distinction between self-love and pride?

Student: No, we can speak of pride as a good thing.

Director: Who has pride in an anarchy?

Student: We'll all have pride, pride in the true and natural sense of the word.

Director: What's the unnatural sense of the word?

Student: Arrogance, the arrogance born of power.

Director: Empire.

Student: Yes.

Director: Anarchy would never have empire, even accidentally?

Student: Never.

Director: Why not?

Student: Because that requires rule, and rule destroys the free soul.

Director: Life-without-rule is about the free soul.

Student: Emphatically, yes.

Director: So you're saying democracy's general will destroys the free soul.

Student: Of course. The soul should be one. In democracy it's many.

Director: Many as in two?

Student: Two is many more than one.

Director: There is the natural soul, and then there is the soul of the general will.

Student: Precisely. The soul in democracy is divided against itself.

Director: Unless we simply don't pay heed to the general will.

Student: Easy to say; hard to do.

Director: But you've done it. Haven't you?

Student: I like to think I have. As have you.

Father: And here I am, the poor man with a divided soul.

Student: The fact that you're letting us have this conversation tells us you aren't as divided as you think.

Director: Or it tells us he's a democrat through and through.

Student: How so?

Director: Democracy allows for many voices. Yes, these voices are thrown into the melting pot and eventually become the general will. But they are voices nonetheless.

Student: My father wants my voice to be melted down into the general will.

Father: I do. This is how you'll educate, my boy—despite yourself.

Student: I don't want to do anything despite myself.

Father: What choice do you have? Some crazy mission to Mars? Educate. Alter the general will for the better. That's the best any of us can hope.

Student: But if we know our voice will be reduced to general will, what incentive do we have to speak pure thoughts?

Director: You're saying, once melted down, thoughts can't be pure?

Student: Of course they can't. They're mixed, blended until unrecognizable. No one of pure thought would ever want that.

Father: The world is mixed; our thoughts should be mixed to match. Anything else is a dream. Pure thought, pure reason—whatever. A dream.

45

Student: If everyone is crazy, should we be crazy, too? What kind of person believes it's better to subordinate their voice to some general will, some sort of averaging of expression of thought?

Father: A person who is aware of the alternatives.

Student: But I'm telling you about a great alternative!

Father: One that would take a huge stroke of luck to achieve. And even then....

Student: Even then what?

Father: I don't have your faith in human nature. I'm sorry, but I don't. Everything turns on your view of human nature. Everything, Son. And I believe it's naive.

Student: And it is naive—naive in the best possible sense. Naive as in not jaded. Naive as in hopeful. Naive as in pure.

Director: Then it's good we have some space for this sort of thing.

Student: What do you mean?

Director: Democracy is not our all. It's our public space. But there is private space here, space where what you're talking about can exist and thrive.

Father: Unlike anarchy.

Student: What do you mean?

Father: Anarchy is, in a way, totalitarian. It permeates everything if it's anything. Democracy has limits.

Student: But the general will doesn't.

Father: You are proof that it does. How can you speak out against the general will if there weren't space allowing for just that? Democracy has limits. It's a compromise. We accept the general will because we're left our space. You've been talking about the general will as if it were all-encompassing. It's not. I, too, am living proof of that. Director is living proof of that.

Director: Student, I must admit your father is speaking sense. Could we have over-stated the power of the general will?

Student: I don't think we have. We three are exceptions that only prove the rule.

Father: I've never liked that easy phrase of proving the rule. How do we prove the rule?

Student: We... we... just do!

Father: No, I think we show that the general will is not as powerful as you thought.

Director: If that's true, it means education toward life-without-rule is possible. The general will might give us space for that. And we can work to move the general will in this direction. Wouldn't that be good?

Student: If it were possible, yes.

Director: Do you see anything wrong with anarcho-democracy? Life with some rule? Isn't that an improvement?

Student: I guess it would be. But how would we reduce the amount of rule in a democracy?

Director: We'd go for the heart. We'd reduce the power of the vote.

Student: How do we do that?

Director: We reduce the power of those who get the votes.

Student: We limit our representatives.

Director: Yes. We narrow their scope.

Student: We let private people decide in their private ways.

Director: Why not?

Student: Rule might just shift to the private, to big corporations and the like. What do we do then?

Director: We give power back to the government.

Student: What, we just go back and forth?

Director: It might work, don't you think? Play the one against the other, back and forth between the two. We never allow one enough time to establish itself in strength.

Student: That... might work.

Director: And if we see openings for life-without-rule, we exploit them.

Student: And none of this means we have to rule out a colony.

Director: Of course not. None of it rules out anything we've had to say.

Father: This sounds like a sensible approach to me.

Student: Me, too. But what if we grow complacent?

Father: Would that we had that as a concern! Do you know what it means to be complacent? It means things are pretty good!

Student: But I don't want pretty good. I want simply good.

Father: Then plant your feet on the pretty good and see what you can do. Just watch out for one thing. Don't make things any worse.

46

Student: How would I do that?

Father: By being a pied piper who leads us down the garden path to our doom. Your quest for anarchy might destroy our democracy.

Student: How? Through education toward life-without-rule? What would that do?

Father: People might lose interest in the issues of the day if they feel their best thoughts are for nothing but melting into the general will.

Student: They feel that way today. A hope for life-without-rule might make them more engaged.

Father: In hopes of breaking away.

Student: Engaged is engaged.

Director: Student, when we're engaged what do we do?

Student: What do you mean?

Director: Do we take decisions into our own hands? Tell the government what to do?

Student: Of course. We pressure our representatives.

Father: That can be a mistake.

Student: Why?

Father: You don't allow the representatives to exercise their expertise.

Student: What expertise? On how to rule?

Father: Expertise on how to keep the peace or win the war.

Student: You're speaking both literally and metaphorically?

Father: Yes.

Student: We can find natural leaders to do these things without the bother of a vote.

Father: All I can say is good luck with that.

Director: Student, do leaders in anarchy rule?

Student: No. They lead. They persuade. They show the way. And people listen.

Father: But the very word 'anarchy' means it all falls apart. Chaos.

Student: That's the oldest prejudice in the world. 'Anarchy is chaos.' It's not. Not even close.

Father: Then when does chaos occur?

Student: Chaos occurs when those who believe in rule realize the rule is bad and they rebel. Anarchists don't believe in rule, so this never happens to them.

Director: Can you say more?

Student: When believers lose their faith, they often panic. And when they panic, there is chaos. Anarchists don't panic. They know rule for what it is. If their rulers let them down, so to speak, they take it in stride.

Director: What do anarchists know rule to be?

Student: Vanity.

Father: Vanity?

Student: Those who rule think they know best. This is vain in the extreme.

Director: But what if they don't think they know best?

Student: Then why would they rule?

Father: You really are very naive. They rule because they think rule is good!

Student: I wouldn't teach them that.

Father: Nietzsche taught that rule is good.

Student: Nietzsche taught a lot of crazy things. Should we have let Nietzsche rule?

Director: Should we let any philosopher rule?

Student: It's not about philosophers. It's about letting anyone rule.

47

Director: A question. Can anyone ever rule in the realm of thought?

Student: Rule another's thought? Yes.

Director: How?

Student: Through fear.

Director: 'Think like me or else'?

Student: That's the size of it.

Director: Is that how the general will works?

Student: That's exactly how it works.

Director: What's the 'or else'?

Student: Ostracism, and all it implies.

Director: But what if it doesn't imply all that much? What if it's merely banishment to the private sphere?

Student: Well... I suppose that wouldn't be all that bad.

Director: And from the private sphere we could continue our education toward life-without-rule?

Student: I don't see why not.

Director: Ostracism might be a blessing in disguise.

Student: True.

Director: And who confers this blessing but the democracy?

Student: It doesn't mean it as a blessing.

Director: How do you know?

Student: It wants... to punish us!

Director: Because it wants to rule?

Student: Yes, of course. All regimes want to rule.

Director: But democracy is relatively benign. It punishes the child by sending it to its room, where it has all means of entertainment at its disposal.

Student: Education toward life-without-rule isn't entertainment.

Director: Oh, I'm not saying it is. I think it's serious. A good thing to do while banished from the realm. You can voice your opinion to any who will listen.

Father: That's the trick. Who will listen? No one en masse.

Director: But does that matter? There will be those who listen. Won't there?

Student: Of course there will.

Director: So life at its worst in democracy isn't so bad.

Student: If that were truly the worst? I'd say that's so.

48

Director: But we want life at its best.

Student: Of course we do.

Director: And we find it in life-without-rule.

Student: Yes.

Director: Tell us. If everyone can't have life-without-rule, is it better for some to have it rather than none?

Student: Of course some is better than none.

Director: What if we had pockets of life-without-rule in a democratic state?

Student: How could we? The democracy would rule despite our best efforts.

Director: What if the democracy doesn't ask much? Don't break the laws and pay your taxes.

Student: Well....

Father: Well what? That isn't asking much.

Student: Alright. Let's say the democracy doesn't ask much.

Director: So pockets of limited life-without-rule might form?

Student: They might.

Director: And some is better than none?

Student: As we've said. But how would we earn a living?

Director: Ah, I thought you might ask. Maybe you grow crops, or make furniture, or devise complex financial products. The point is—you do something on your own. Isn't that what life-without-rule is all about?

Student: Doing something on your own? I never put it that way before. But I guess it is.

Director: And 'on your own' might be one alone—a writer. Or it might be a hundred together—those harvesting crops. Or a team of financial experts. Whatever. The point is you rely on yourselves.

Student: You rely on the market for your services or goods.

Director: Do you have a problem with markets? I know of many anarcho-capitalists.

Student: Markets are a sort of general will.

Director: Okay. But without them, how would you earn a living?

Student: I don't know.

Director: I know how. If I'm an expert at pouring foundations, and you're an expert framer, might we not work together on the construction of a house?

Student: Sure.

Director: And do we need a 'market' in order for someone to buy our house?

Student: No, we don't need a market in order for someone to buy our house. It just takes one person.

Director: So that, or something like it, is how we'd earn our living. What should we call this?

Student: The natural economy.

Director: Sounds good to me. Can we grow the natural economy within the private sphere of democracy?

Student: We can.

Director: Is there any rule within the natural economy?

Student: No, there are only people helping each other get what they want.

Director: Do we have to do away with money?

Student: I don't think we do.

Director: Are you sure? Doesn't money represent a kind of rule?

Student: I know what you mean. But it's more of a convenience, a facilitator, than a type of rule.

Director: Will we have massive central banks?

Student: No, of course not. At most we'd have agreed upon value at the local level.

Director: What would we call our currency?

Student: Oh, I don't know.

Director: What if we call it the student, after its founder? A hundred students buys you a house.

Student: No, that's ridiculous. We can think of a name later.

Director: Alright. But will the democracy be jealous of our local success?

Student: Maybe not—if we don't toot our own horn.

49

Director: And that's in keeping with the faith.

Student: What do you mean?

Director: Anarchy isn't raucous. It's a quiet affair.

Student: Life-without-rule is peaceful, yes.

Director: Do you know why I like a quiet state of peace?

Student: Because you're at peace in your soul.

Director: Because reason is best heard in such a state.

Student: And reason brings us peace in our soul.

Director: Reason that's listened to, yes. Reason is often drowned out in the noise of democracy. But not in the quiet spheres that exist.

Student: True, like here. But what if the whole world were a quiet sphere?

Father: I don't think most of the world, especially the young, want quiet. Many want excitement and noise.

Student: Noise and excitement are fine as long as they're exceptions to the rule.

Father: Rule?

Student: You know what I mean.

Father: I'm starting to think anarchy might be boring.

Student: Well, I'll take that as a win.

Father: What do you mean?

Student: Anarchy went from terrifying to boring. Better the latter any day.

Director: What would people do in life-without-rule?

Student: For one, they'd work to make a living. And when they're done with that they'd enjoy each other's company.

Director: What would they talk about?

Student: What do we talk about now? Remember, interesting people are never bored.

Director: Is that why democracy relies on spectacles? Because people aren't interesting?

Student: If the shoe fits....

Director: But this is a problem, isn't it?

Student: How so?

Director: Suppose an anarchy evolves. What would the uninteresting former democrats do but cause trouble?

Father: Oh, you're missing the point, Director. Without the general will to keep them down, they would be interesting!

Student: I know you're teasing, but it's true. Without the general will to interfere, people's true personalities come out. And true personality never bores.

Director: I'll take that as a sort of faith in humanity.

Student: And it is.

Director: If we're wrong about humanity, about human nature—will anarchy be a terrible mistake?

Student: If we're wrong, an anarchy can't evolve.

Director: And if we set one up all at once, as with the colony?

Student: The colonists will be forced to fall back toward rule.

Father: That sounds very neat and clean. But if we're wrong about human nature we'll have anarchy-in-the-bad-old-sense. You can't dismantle government and expect to put the genie back in the bottle when things go bad.

Student: But if we start to see that things are bad—

Father: Oh, you might not see until it's much too late. You'll get people to believe they'll do well in life-without-rule. But put them in it, have them live it— and you might be in for a terrible surprise.

Director: How do we recover from such a mistake?

Father: I think it would take a sort of dictatorship to right the ship. And over a long period of time we might evolve toward democracy again. Or so we can hope. There's no guarantee.

Director: So you're basically saying, we have it pretty good; don't mess it up.

Father: That's exactly what I'm saying. But the young can't always appreciate this, what we have. They always want more.

Student: You can both appreciate and want more. I appreciate our democracy. It's the best form of government existing in the world today.

Father: How can you say that with all you've said about the general will?

Student: The general will becomes a problem once other needs are met.

Father: And you're betting anarchy can meet those needs.

Student: Life-without-rule, yes.

Director: Do you think of it as something like this? Democracy is a set of training wheels for the human sprit as it learns to ride.

Student: Yes, I like that. There is nothing wrong with training wheels. But at a certain point we want them off. The youth of today are learning to ride.

Director: How do they learn?

Student: They experiment in little things.

Director: Like their interpersonal relationships?

Student: Definitely. Habits formed there carry over into other things.

Director: So we can't rule our friends.

Student: We can't.

Director: Let's be sure. What does it mean to rule a friend?

Student: It means to be domineering, in however an attenuated sense.

Director: It means to exert your will?

Student: Yes.

Director: Can we live without a will?

Student: We should will ourselves, not others.

Director: Self-rule?

Student: Well, that's an interesting question. Is there self-rule in life-without-rule?

Director: Is there?

Student: I don't know. I'm asking you.

Director: This is a very big question. I don't have the answer. Father?

Father: Don't ask me. I'm opposed to the whole thing. All I know is that in democracy, self-rule is critical to our success.

Director: What is self-rule?

Father: Moderation in all things.

Director: Student?

Student: I can go along with that. How about you?

Director: I'd say it's moderation in all things except for thought.

Father: Why thought?

Director: We need to be as precise yet wide ranging as can be. That takes constant effort.

Student: That makes sense. But here's the problem I have. In life-without-rule our appetites will be moderate as a matter of course. The general will won't urge us on. Given that, we'll have no need for self-rule.

Director: What about the things we say? Do we just blurt out whatever we think?

Student: Yes.

Father: Ha!

Student: We'll have evolved to such a state that thoughts won't give offense.

Father: Fantasy talk again.

Student: Maybe there are stages to life-without-rule. In the first stage, we might have to regulate our speech. But as we proceed, we open up.

51

Director: Just imagine. Saying whatever we think without fear of consequences.

Father: Yes, I am imagining—and I don't like what I see!

Student: When I imagine this I see everyone happy, happy and free.

Father: Even if someone is wrong about you?

Student: What do you mean?

Director: What if someone says they think you're a coward? Would that make you happy?

Student: Of course not. But they wouldn't say it.

Director: Why not?

Student: Because I'm not a coward.

Director: So life-without-rule makes us see truth?

Student: It's easier to see truth without the general will in the way.

Director: What about someone who is a coward? Would you call them that?

Father: Wait. Don't tell me. There will be no cowards in life-without-rule. There will be no liars in life without rule. In fact, there won't even be those who like to embellish the truth!

Student: It's true.

Father: Ha! We'll be living in a perfect world. Rule is the source of all our ills.

Student: Why is that so hard for you to believe?

Father: Because it goes against everything I know.

Student: What you know you see through the lens of rule. You see people unhappy because of rule and you assume people must always be that way.

Father: Then how do you explain those who are happy?

Student: They only seem happy.

Father: How would you know?

Student: I have friends who are 'happy'. They're mostly miserable inside.

Father: And you really think that's because of rule?

Student: That's the one thing they all have in common.

Father: They all breathe air. They have that in common, too.

Director: Student, how does rule make us unhappy?

Student: Our laws are made to fit a sort of average person. But no such average person exists. So the laws don't fit anyone well. Some better than others, sure. But no one well.

Director: And we need well fitting laws to make us happy?

Student: We need life-without-rule to make us happy.

Father: So we run around naked without any law.

Director: Why not focus your efforts, Student, on making democratic laws fit better? That might not make us perfectly happy, but wouldn't it make us less unhappy?

Student: Yes, but fit whom? The population fits into a bell curve on most things. Few on the extremes; many in the middle. Do we just focus on the middle?

Director: Haven't you considered that bell curves derive from the general will?

Student: That's an excellent point! So what should we do?

Director: While the bell curves still exist, make laws that take them into account.

Student: Those on the extremes have different laws than those in the middle?

Director: Sure. We do it today with taxes, for instance. Why not generalize the practice?

Student: But if the laws fit better, won't they be stronger?

Director: Maybe. But people might suffer less from the general will.

52

Father: But what does this do to equality before the law?

Director: We all must obey the law, whichever law applies.

Father: And who will fashion these laws?

Director: Lawmakers will rely on experts.

Father: Experts in what?

Director: Enhanced census data and the like.

Father: You really want the government to gather all sorts of data on us?

Director: How else to get a better fit? But, Student, what do you think? Is this a step closer to life-without-rule? Or is it a step in the wrong direction?

Student: If it can lessen the ill effect of the general will, it's a step in the right direction.

Director: What's the next step after this?

Student: I... don't know.

Director: Well, what if we stop enforcement of the laws?

Student: Let them be guidelines?

Director: Yes.

Father: Ha, ha! 'We suggest you pay your taxes.' That will work well.

Student: We could publish a list of who pays what.

Father: And you'll shame people into paying?

Student: Why not?

Father: Isn't that a sort of general will, that shame?

Student: Yes, but it's better than a law. It might be more effective, too.

Director: What's the next step after this?

Student: We get rid of the guidelines. People pay what they want.

Father: No one will pay!

Student: We'll still publish who pays what.

Father: Let me guess. The final step is to stop publishing the list.

Student: Yes. No shame or pride in the matter—just what needs to be done.

Father: People will pay out of self-interest?

Student: People do all sorts of things out of self-interest. Why not this? Besides, we won't have a culture where people hide their money.

Father: Everyone will know everyone's business?

Student: Why not?

Director: What about personal business?

Student: What sort of business do you have in mind?

Director: Affairs of the heart.

Student: There will be nothing to hide.

Father: Will there be marriages?

Student: No.

Director: Why not?

Student: We don't need vows that rule us. We'll stay true on our own, because we want to.

Father: Romantic anarchy. Well, I wish you luck. A lot of trouble would pass from the world if things can work as you think.

53

Director: Student, I wonder what would happen if things don't turn out the way you expect.

Student: How so?

Director: What if human nature is other than you think? And not bad, no. But different.

Student: I would have to adjust. We would all have to adjust.

Director: Why would we have to adjust? Nature is nature.

Student: But when we think it's other than it is, we form habits around what we think.

Director: Bad habits.

Student: Yes.

Director: And those bad habits are sometimes supported by laws.

Student: Of course.

Director: Laws and habits are hard to change.

Student: That's why a gradual evolution toward life-without-rule might be best.

Director: Do you see this as inevitable?

Student: Why do you keep asking me that? No. People will resist.

Director: What sort of people?

Student: People who think they benefit from the old ways.

Father: Think? The rich don't know they benefit from the old ways?

Student: Not all of them. In fact, the very rich and the very poor might be the first to espouse the cause.

Director: Why?

Student: The very rich can afford to experiment. The very poor have nothing to lose.

Director: So the middle class will resist with the most force.

Student: Yes.

Director: How do you help them evolve? Courses on life-without-rule like the one you're in?

Student: Well, the course is really about democracy.

Father: That's because it's hard to get a course on anarchy onto the curriculum. Parents like me wouldn't care for that much.

Student: Courses like mine can help.

Director: Because the students come out of them with more open minds?

Student: They tend to, yes. But not all of them do. Some of them make fun of the professor outside of class.

Director: What do they say?

Student: That he's crazy. That he has his head in the clouds. That he really just wants to be free to be amoral.

Director: Is life-without-rule amoral?

Student: Yes. Morals are a form of rule.

Father: And I pay for this course.

Director: Are they a form of self-rule or a sort of rule by others?

Student: It depends. Some rule themselves with moral principles; others obey only because of the threat of force.

Director: But in life-without-rule no one desires to do anything immoral?

Student: They don't.

Director: So natural desire is benign.

Student: Not only is it benign, it's actually good. Good for the person; good for others.

Director: What happens to someone with natural desire under the general will?

Student: Their desires are crushed.

Director: Always?

Student: There are a few who satisfy them once in a while. I think you're one of them.

Director: I am? How so?

Student: What's your greatest desire?

Director: To have conversations like this.

Student: And you have them.

Director: Not as often as I'd like.

Student: Still, you have them from time to time. How do you feel when you do?

Director: Like a fish in water.

Student: In life-without-rule you could have these conversations every day.

Director: I don't know, Student.

Student: Why couldn't you?

Director: Because men are men and not fish.

54

Student: What's that supposed to mean?

Director: I don't know. It sounded good, didn't it? But, seriously, I'm starting to think all or none will be philosophers in life-without-rule. What if it's none?

Student: It would only be none if philosophy is not a natural desire.

Director: Do you believe it's a natural desire?

Student: Have you always been a philosopher, or was there a time before?

Director: If there was, I don't recall. Is that how it goes for all natural desires? There was never a time before?

Student: Yes.

Father: Oh, this is ridiculous. Think of sexual desire. We all had a time before. Are we saying sexual desire isn't natural?

Director: He has a point.

Student: Maybe it isn't natural.

Father: Ha! I'm getting a lot of good laughs for my money today.

Student: Older people lose their desire, don't they?

Father: Some but not all.

Student: Are they happier for it?

Father: Well, I suppose it's less tormenting.

Student: How can something that torments us be natural?

Director: You think the torment is a function of rule?

Student: Yes. Sex and power always get mixed when there is rule.

Director: He may have a point.

Father: Yes, he very well may.

Director: So are we saying there is no power in life-without-rule?

Student: What power would there be? Power and rule are one.

Director: Then sex in life-without-rule is, at most, just a gentle desire?

Student: I think it is. No one suffers agonies of longing over this.

Father: Everything in life-without-rule is mild.

Student: What's wrong with that?

Father: There is no zest.

Student: There is happiness.

Father: What kind of happiness?

Student: Do you remember how much fun you had as a child at play? That's what every day would be like.

Director: The world constantly opens before us?

Student: Yes! There are always things to discover.

Father: But what's to discover when everyone is the same?

Student: Why do you think they'd be the same?

Father: Differences in power differentiate one from another.

Student: You've read too much Nietzsche, Dad.

Director: What differentiates those in life-without-rule?

Student: Little things, that aren't so little. That's the best I can say.

55

Director: There's something I'm still wondering, Student. Will people be equal in life-without-rule?

Student: Of course.

Director: Hmm. But isn't equality a democratic thing?

Student: Are you wondering if it's an offshoot of the general will?

Director: Is it?

Student: Well, equality has to do with our relationship to power. Without that relationship, our need for equality is gone. And this is good. Without equality to blind us, we can focus on and appreciate and enjoy natural differences.

Father: Natural differences? That's a source of trouble.

Student: Why would you say that?

Father: Haven't you ever heard of loyalty to one's own? Like will align with like, and conflict will arise.

Student: Haven't you ever heard that opposites attract? Opposites and one's own will cancel each other, I think.

Father: No, I think you're going to have lots of trouble with the opposites that attract.

Student: How so?

Father: Think of the 360 degrees along a circle. Each has an opposite across a diameter. That makes 180 pairs. What stops these 180 from resenting one another as they criss cross back and forth?

Student: Why would they resent one another?

Father: They all have to pass through the center on their way to their paired opposite. There will be congestion. This will cause frustrations. Petty episodes will soon build into full blown conflict.

Student: Oh, you're being ridiculous. This won't happen in life-without-rule.

Father: That's your answer for everything. But you don't account for daily frictions that over time can irritate even the best of human nature.

Director: Can there be life-without-rule with these frictions? In other words, do they get so bad that they necessitate a kind of rule?

Father: That's my opinion. Better to have a democracy, with all its imperfections, than violent anarchy.

Director: If we find ourselves in violent anarchy, what can we do?

Father: Find a good king to bring order to things. Only we probably wouldn't call this person a king, or queen.

Director: What would we call them? An executive?

Father: I don't know. Something like that. But this would be rule with a vengeance in order to straighten things out.

Director: How long before we come back around to democracy?

Father: Centuries. Millennia. I don't know. But we won't see it in our lifetime.

Director: Why not?

Father: The people will be corrupt from fighting each other. There will be hard feelings that last. In such a state democracy doesn't work.

Director: Why?

Father: Because people won't abide by the majority decisions. In order for that to happen, there must be a modicum of respect for those with the votes. It goes the other way, too. The majority must respect the minority, not take pleasure in crushing it.

Director: But in executive rule there is no need for respect?

Father: Oh, respect always makes things better. The point is that an executive can rule when there is none.

Director: What's the character of executive rule when there is none?

Father: It will be harsh. There will be no tolerance for disobedience.

Student: There will be no tolerance for speaking out against the government?

Father: None, if the people are really corrupt. The executive can't afford for them to be inflamed. They're already inflamed against each other.

Director: When things are so far gone, is executive rule the only thing that can prevent a civil war?

Father: Yes. It takes concentration of power in order to stop, or win, such a thing.

Director: But a corrupt people won't just vote an executive in. It must have no choice.

Father: The truth is it must be sick of war.

Director: But are we talking about a real guns and bullets war? Or is this political warfare?

Father: I wish it could be the latter, but I doubt it. The political warfare would have to be really, really bad—enough to wake the people to the need for concentration of power.

56

Director: I wonder if there's a way to combine life-without-rule with concentration of power.

Student: Impossible. How would something like that even look?

Director: The people would have to choose someone they implicitly trust, someone with a love for life-without-rule.

Student: If the person loves life-without-rule, why would they take up rule?

Director: Because it would save life-without-rule for others.

Student: But this makes no sense. Taking up rule would destroy life-without-rule for others.

Director: It would have to be a very limited rule.

Student: Limited to what?

Director: Keeping the peace.

Student: So the executive will simply break up fights?

Director: Yes, mercilessly.

Father: I think Director has a point. Anarchy will have a real need for this.

Student: What's to stop the executive from exercising his or her will on other things?

Director: Self-interest.

Student: Please explain.

Director: Do you think rule is bad for the ruler?

Student: I do.

Director: Why would anyone want to do something that's bad for them?

Student: They... wouldn't.

Director: So why would a limited ruler want to take on more rule?

Student: I don't know. But it's happened in the past.

Father: It's happened in the past? Ha! You make it sound as if this weren't the universal rule! People who get a taste of power always want more.

Student: Not always.

Director: That 'not always' is what we need. What do you think it takes?

Student: They look forward to stepping down more than they do to climbing up.

Director: It has to be someone who truly doesn't want to rule. How can we prove them before we place them on high?

Father: Prove them all you want. People change when they come to power.

Director: How so?

Father: There's nothing as satisfying as the exercise of power.

Director: How would you know?

Father: I exercise power every day.

Director: At your company.

Father: Yes, and in the political work I do.

Director: You're a sort of kingmaker in the party.

Father: I am. No one runs for office in this county without coming through me.

Director: You've seen people change?

Father: I have. And that's why we need balances and checks.

Director: What balance is there in an anarchy with an executive?

Student: It's all the people against one woman or man.

Father: What about their executive apparatus, those who will enforce the executive's will?

Student: The people will enforce the will—provided the rule isn't too strong.

Director: What if the executive will is too strong?

Student: The people will force him or her out.

Director: So the executive can retake their place in the life-without-rule?

Student: No, they will be banished. Fear of that will help keep them in check.

Director: Do you think a limited term of office would also help keep them in check?

Student: I think that's the only way you could get someone to rule.

Director: Because life-without-rule is so sweet.

Student: Yes. They'll want to behave during their term so they can take it up again.

Director: So rule in life-without-rule is a joyless duty?

Student: That puts it well.

Director: What if the ruler stays within bounds but finds rule to be satisfying, as your father was saying?

Student: We remove that ruler from rule.

Director: But what if in finding rule satisfying he or she does a better job? Isn't that a sort of gift? You'll still have your balances and checks to ensure there's no trouble.

Student: Yes, but it's a form of corruption that sets a bad example.

57

Director: You mean others will learn to want to rule.

Student: Yes, especially the impressionable young.

Director: They'll see that rule is pleasant and want it for themselves.

Student: No, Director. Rule is never pleasant.

Director: What do you mean?

Student: We spoke of a ruler finding rule to be satisfying, not pleasant. Satisfaction differs from pleasure. Rule is never pleasant.

Director: Father?

Father: He has a point.

Director: Do people always prefer satisfaction over pleasure?

Father: No, not always.

Director: When do they?

Father: When they're trapped.

Director: I don't understand. Are you saying that people who come to power are trapped?

Father: Yes.

Director: And you're a sort of trapper?

Father: I am.

Student: How can you be proud of that?

Father: I take satisfaction in it.

Director: Because you, too, are trapped.

Father: We're all trapped to a certain degree.

Student: I'm not.

Father: You will be, once you have to earn a living. And this is where you're naive. The people in life-without-rule will have to make a living. They will be trapped. And when you're trapped, changes seem good.

Director: Political changes.

Father: Yes. How do you think elections work?

Student: But people will enjoy their work!

Father: Says someone who's never had to work. Try it for fifty years and see what you think.

Student: I intend to find interesting work.

Father: At best you'll end up with satisfying work.

Director: That doesn't sound so bad.

Father: No, but rule is the only satisfying work there is. It comes in many forms. I rule at work; I rule in politics. So do many others. Democracy gives them a taste. That's what makes it work.

Student: But satisfaction in rule is a form of corruption!

Father: Was Abraham Lincoln corrupt? He took satisfaction in rule.

Student: How do you know?

Father: He was eager for the job. And in those terrible times of civil war, he needed something to sustain him.

Student: He had faith.

Father: Sure he had faith. Faith in our democracy. Faith in his ability to lead our democracy. And as he led, as he ruled, he found enough satisfaction along the way to sustain him in his task.

Director: Can anyone live without satisfaction?

Father: It happens. Little pleasures can make up life.

Director: As can little satisfactions?

Father: Of course.

Student: You're describing a world of petty rule.

Father: Don't you think that's better than a life of magnificent rule?

58

Director: Magnificence. Is that something missing from life-without-rule?

Student: Magnificence is overrated. No, we'll have no magnificence. But we will have wonderful deeds.

Director: Like writing a symphony?

Student: Or a book, sure. And so on.

Director: How about serving a good term as an executive?

Father: I think you deserve some praise for that. Don't you agree?

Student: The problem with praise is that youth will often want to emulate the one who's praised.

Director: Is that a general problem or one limited to the executive and the like?

Student: It's a general problem. Let's say you're praised for your part in a play. Certain youths will very much want to play a praise-winning role as well.

Father: What's wrong with that?

Student: They'll want this even if they're not very good.

Director: Acting isn't their thing.

Student: Exactly. Praise of others distracts them from what they ought to do, ought to be.

Director: They have the idea of the thing but not the thing itself.

Student: Just so.

Director: Is it possible to have the idea of rule but not rule itself?

Student: People might dream about rule and have no idea of the true burden it is.

Father: There's only one way to know—and then they're trapped.

Student: But no one is trapped in life-without-rule. An executive can step down at any time.

Father: I don't think it's that simple. Don't you know there's such a thing as pride? Your executive would be performing a service to the community. Stepping down would be hard, a failure.

Student: Failure to rule is no blemish.

Father: Failure to save the community is. Or don't you think that's what the executive does? An executive is called on in a time of need, right?

Student: True.

Father: Who likes to fail in a time of need? And isn't it an honor to be chosen?

Student: I'm not sure we should think of it as an honor. After all, no one wants the job.

Father: But someone must do it.

Student: I can tell how much you enjoy this problem of an executive in life-without-rule.

Director: Student, how would the crisis come about that necessitates an executive?

Student: An overwhelming accident could cause it, I suppose.

Director: Bad luck?

Student: Sure, bad luck.

Director: And what if the luck is so bad that people don't want to listen to an executive?

Student: I guess there's nothing to be done.

Director: But chances are they'll know their interest and listen?

Student: That's a good point. In a crisis people will know they have to be open to persuasion by an executive.

Father: Persuasion? Won't that take too long? Decisions have to be made, and adhered to, quickly in a crisis.

Student: You don't think the community knows that? Everyone knows that. It's in everyone's interest to coordinate quickly. In fact, now that I think of it, rule here would slow things down.

59

Father: How?

Student: Rule changes patterns of interest. Some people align with the rule and not the community. This creates inefficiencies, to put it mildly.

Director: What would make someone misalign?

Student: A mistake.

Father: What mistake?

Student: A mistake that... that....

Director: It wouldn't be a mistake, would it?

Student: They would mistake their interests.

Director: They would be attracted to power.

Student: Well... yes.

Director: So human nature isn't perfect? Some of us are attracted to power, some aren't?

Student: I guess that's true.

Director: And this is by nature?

Father: We're all attracted by nature!

Student: No, most of us aren't. Most of us want peaceful existence. Only some want trouble.

Director: But could it be a function of nurture rather than nature?

Student: Our nature in some ways determines our nurture.

Father: That's true.

Director: So our life-without-rule will have some that want trouble. Should we kick them out as soon as they're unmasked?

Student: That's the only sensible thing to do.

Father: Tell me something, Son. Where do these people go?

Student: They go.... I don't know.

Father: Will they resent being kicked out?

Student: I'm sure some of them will. But they're mistaken in this.

Director: They're mistaken in what they feel?

Student: No, they feel what they feel. But being kicked out is a benefit to them.

Director: Because they can go to a place where rule is good?

Student: Where it's thought to be good. Yes.

Director: Might they not persuade their new friends to turn on life-without-rule?

Student: Attack us?

Director: Their being there increases the risk, don't you think?

Student: That risk is always there, no matter whom we kick out. Assuming, of course, life-without-rule isn't global.

Father: But it can never be global. There will always be those who by nature align with rule. They will band together. And don't worry, you won't have to kick all of these people out. Many of them will leave of their own accord.

Director: So if ten percent of humans align by nature with rule, at most ninety percent of the world's people can live life-without-rule. Are we all agreed on this?

Father: Agreed, though I think the numbers should be reversed.

Student: I can agree to the original numbers.

Director: Okay. But what about the colony? What if we send only those who align by nature with life-without-rule? Might a world not grow up around them free of rule?

Father: Maybe for a single generation. But after that, all bets are off.

60

Director: Because of changes in nature? Mutations? The general oddities of heredity?

Father: Yes, of course.

Student: But nurture can go a very long way.

Director: What's the cardinal rule of nurture in life-without-rule?

Student: Never praise rule.

Father: So we have to rewrite all the history books?

Student: If we did, we'd rewrite them from the perspective of life-without-rule.

Father: So you don't believe in heroes.

Student: Of course I do—everyday heroes, not glorious leader heroes.

Director: What's an example of an everyday hero?

Student: Someone who saves a child from a fire. There's no rule in that.

Director: No, certainly not. And we praise this person, with the hope that others will emulate them?

Student: We no doubt do.

Director: So if people have ambition, regardless of whether all people have ambition, we want to steer them toward deeds like this.

Student: Yes.

Father: But those with real ambition, all consuming ambition, won't be satisfied with this.

Director: Is ambition necessarily linked to rule?

Father: It is.

Student: Then out they go.

Father: And if another rises to take their place? And then another? And another?

Student: We'll.... We'll.... I don't know.

Director: Tell us, Father. What do the ambitious want?

Father: Power.

Student: No, I think they want fame.

Director: Are hunger for power and thirst for fame different things?

Student: You can be thirsty for fame and allow that to lead you to a life of discovery in science, for instance. You can hunger for power and be a behind-the-scenes kingmaker, who never obtains fame—for instance.

Director: Father?

Father: I don't thirst for fame. But I do like power.

Director: Are you ambitious?

Father: Yes.

Student: If you were ambitious for fame you'd be more honest.

Father: Would I? Why?

Student: Because everyone could see what you're about.

Father: Maybe. But power is more reliable than fame.

Student: How so?

Father: Power makes no false moves. Fame is all over the place. Power is calculating, steady, incremental. Fame is a wild goose chase for opinion.

Director: Fame really is all about opinion, isn't it?

Father: Of course it is.

Student: But so is power.

Director: How so?

Student: If you're thought to be more powerful than you are, you're more powerful than you are. If you're thought to be less powerful than you are, you're less powerful than you are. Does that make sense?

Father: I'll admit it makes sense to me. Even behind the scenes, where I operate, what people think of you counts.

Director: Why isn't that fame?

Father: Because fame is what everyone thinks. Power is what those who matter think.

Director: In a democracy everyone matters, no?

Student: In life-without-rule everyone matters even more.

Father: Why do they matter more?

Student: Because they're not deceived by rule. They're clear in mind.

Father: Democrats aren't clear in mind? Do you really want to say this now, to the greatest democracy there has ever been? The greatest power there ever has been?

Student: Democrats could be better. That's what I say. They need to take the next step. They need to begin shedding the layers of rule.

61

Director: How do they do that?

Father: Yes, what layer is on top?

Student: It's not the top we must shed. It's the bottom.

Father: How do you shed a bottom layer? It makes no sense.

Student: It makes sense if you consider it going forward.

Director: So what's at bottom?

Student: I'm surprised you haven't guessed from what we just said. Praise for rule.

Father: Do you really think today's politicians are so highly praised?

Student: They're not—because we hold very high standards for rule, and begrudgingly make do with what we've got.

Director: Then where's the praise?

Student: With leaders from the past.

Director: Why do you think people praise them highly?

Student: Because it's easy to forget the bad side to their good.

Director: How do we stop this praise for the past?

Student: There's only one way—through education toward life-without-rule.

Father: Yes, yes, only one way. But, Son, I can live without praise—and I will rule, nonetheless.

Student: But don't you want to be a hero?

Father: A hero? Ha, ha. What are you talking about?

Director: What makes for a hero, Student?

Student: Sacrifice.

Father: What kind of sacrifice?

Student: Sacrifice of ambition.

Father: And to whom will that make me a hero?

Student: Your family.

Father: How?

Student: Your ambition is in the way of your progress toward life-without-rule. Your lack of progress hinders the progress of the family.

Father: You seem to be progressing very well.

Student: Yes, but it's despite your rule. Besides, wouldn't you rather be less of an enigma?

Father: Enigma? What are you talking about?

Student: Power—rule—cloaks your true self. It has to.

Director: Why does it have to, Student?

Student: Because rule always makes you more than you are.

Director: Is your father more than he is? He is, after all, a ruler in his sphere.

Student: His sphere being business and politics? Yes, he's more than he is.

Father: That doesn't make any sense.

Student: The positions you hold give you power disproportionate to what force you could project all on your own.

Director: Are you saying he enjoys business and political infrastructures that magnify his rule?

Student: Precisely. And it's especially bad with politics because the party apparatus limits choice.

Father: Yes it does. And that's a good thing.

Student: It takes us further away from life-without-rule.

Director: Why does it do that, Student?

Student: Because the parties introduce a layer of rule. The people rule. The parties rule. And then the elected rule.

Director: If we remove the parties, does more rule fall to the people and their elected leaders?

Student: I... think it does.

Director: Overall, it's the same amount of rule?

Father: I like what you're saying, Director. Parties reduce the concentration of rule.

Student: That's... a joke!

Father: Joke or not, it's true.

Student: The ultimate dilution of rule is for it to be entirely in the people's hands. Direct democracy. And then the next step—though it's darkest before the dawn, because of the power of the general will—is life-without-rule.

62

Director: In a direct democracy, does rule dilute further as the people grow in number? In other words, is there less rule when there are 10,000 people than when there are 1,000?

Student: Well, rule is rule. But each individual has less rule the greater the population.

Director: And that's good?

Student: Less rule is better, yes.

Director: So democracy needs to expand.

Student: I suppose. But I don't like the notion of conquest.

Father: But what if the democracy conquers the rulers of a people, a non-democratic people, but not that people itself?

Student: Well, that's better. And it makes the people citizens?

Father: Yes.

Student: Then I'm alright with that.

Father: Good. But I think we need to clear something up.

Student: What?

Father: What you said about dilution of rule.

Student: What was wrong with what I said?

Father: It was the opposite of the truth.

Student: What's the truth?

Father: To rule over 1,000 people involves a certain amount of rule, x. To rule over 10,000 people involves $10x$. Rule doesn't dilute.

Student: Even if that's true, a greater population is better.

Father: Why?

Student: Haven't you ever heard of losing yourself in the crowd?

Director: Student, you mentioned that the next step from direct democracy is life-without-rule. When is that step most likely? When there are few democrats or many?

Student: Many, because then the rule is—despite what my father thinks—so dilute the change won't be a shock.

Director: So 1,000,000 are more likely to cross over than 10,000.

Student: Maybe we should say that with a greater population more are more likely to cross over, but not all at once.

Director: Why not?

Student: That would take a huge amount of luck.

Director: What kind of luck?

Student: They'd need a nudge, something that encourages them to take the step. You know how people are.

Director: But if life-without-rule is as wonderful as you say, what would stop them?

Student: Anything new is frightening, Director.

Father: They need to be lured into life-without-rule.

Director: Lured? How?

Father: With the oldest bait in the book—money. We need to play to their greed.

Student: No! Greed is the death of life-without-rule.

Director: Why especially greed?

Student: Greed prevents people from making pure decisions. Nothing corrupts like greed.

Director: I thought there wouldn't be greed in life-without-rule. I thought you'd say it's a perversion born of rule.

Student: Yes, but we shouldn't invite it in!

Father: I don't think it's always born of rule. Greed can be by nature, too.

Director: Student?

Student: Let's say it's... possible.

Director: So in life-without-rule we would kick the greedy-by-nature out?

Student: Yes.

Father: We might do a lot of kicking out.

Student: Better that than the alternative.

Director: And if we find greed that was created by rule?

Student: When the rule is gone, the lust is, too.

Director: You said greed causes bad decisions. What's the effect of these decisions?

Student: People don't get what they by nature want.

Father: Ha! By nature they want money!

Director: What do they by nature want, Student?

Student: The good ones want simple things. Fellowship, love, pleasant activities. Simple.

Director: Why can't they have those things in a corrupt society? I have them now and I live here, assuming 'here' is corrupt.

Father: Yes, Student. Why?

Student: Director, you're an exception. Most people can't find those things. Why not? Because they're drinking from a poisoned well.

Father: What well?

Student: Society. It puts pressure on them to want other things.

Father: What, are you talking about ads?

Student: Ads, sure. They're part of the general will. They both shape and are shaped by it. An awful circle of greed.

Father: Oh, I don't know. Sometimes ads make me smile. And sometimes they encourage me to buy something I really enjoy. You make them sound sinister.

Student: They're sinister when they distort your view. When your view is distorted, you can't see well enough to find friends to love and enjoy. You lose focus on the simple joys in life.

Father: So this is your great big bogeyman? Pressure to acquire?

Student: No! It's much worse than that. Rule pressures us to obey, in the broadest possible sense.

Father: 'Obey'? Why can't you say 'listen'?

Student: We can say 'listen'. But 'obey' gives a better sense of what's involved.

Director: Tell us more.

Student: When you have to obey, you can't do as you like.

Father: Profound.

Student: Over time this causes a sort of resentment to build.

Father: Yes, we all resent not being able to do whatever we like.

Student: The resentment becomes chronic. And when it does, we can't think clearly. And if we can't think clearly, we can't focus on simple things like finding our friends.

Father: We can find our brothers in resentment, I suppose. That's a good second best, no?

Student: I can't tell if you're serious or not. Maybe you can't, either.

Director: What do these brothers do?

Student: I think they seek rule.

Director: Why?

Student: They sense rule is crucial here, but they don't know why. And they seek it not knowing what it is.

Father: Poor devils.

Director: And when they find it, Student?

Student: It's too late.

63

Father: They're trapped.

Student: Yes, but not in the way you think. They're trapped because they've wasted their lives chasing a phantom. And if they didn't cause so much harm, it would be sad.

Director: What harm do they cause?

Student: They make others believe rule must be good.

Director: Why isn't it good?

Student: Well, what is rule?

Director: I suppose most would say it's control over others.

Student: What would you say?

Director: 'Control' might be too strong a word. Not all rule is simply control.

Student: What word would be just right?

Director: I don't know if it's just right, but 'sway' seems good. Rule is sway over others. Father, what do you think?

Father: I like 'sway'. I don't control would-be candidates. I hold sway over them.

Director: How do you sway others?

Father: I make them aware of the facts.

Director: That sounds good. And the facts tell them what to do?

Father: Yes, very clearly.

Student: Sure, but one of the facts is your will. You make them aware of that. And you make them aware of the wills of other powerful men.

Father: Will is a fact. What can I say?

Student: This will is at the heart of rule. What is rule? Rule is will, the imposition of will.

Director: Rule of self, rule over others—it doesn't matter? Rule is will?

Student: Rule is will.

Director: So there will be no will in life-without-rule?

Student: Will is a dangerous thing. Its abuse is the source of most of the trouble in this world.

Father: You'd have us clip the tiger's claws.

Student: And make us less terrible than we are? I'd say yes, but for the fact that humans aren't born with claws.

Father: Some of them are born aggressive, no? Would they, too, be kicked out of your life-without-rule?

Student: We have no place for aggression—or passivity, for that matter.

Director: Why not passivity?

Student: Passivity is a form of corruption. It's a failure to live your life as it should be led.

Father: In a place with no rule, you're going to tell people how their lives should be led?

Student: No, but we're not going to encourage people to rot. They have to take a healthy interest in life.

Father: And if they don't, do you kick them out?

Student: Yes. We have to get rid of the rotten apples before the rot spreads.

Father: Your little anarchy is starting to sound like quite the exclusive club. Who decides which apples are bad?

Student: It's a problem, yes. Problems are part of life.

Father: Maybe you should decide by consensus, a sort of general will. Or maybe a standing executive decides. Or—

Student: I take the point.

Director: But doesn't everything ride on this point? In life-without-rule the community is all.

Student: It is. I just don't have an answer. We'll have to figure it out along the way. Unless you have something in mind.

Director: What if we simply make it very easy for people to leave? If you have frustrated ambition, or it bothers you that everyone is too active, or whatever—we have a fund for your relocation.

Student: We help set them up in another life elsewhere?

Director: At no charge to them.

Father: And with no dishonor?

Director: None from us. And their new found home will welcome them as those who've seen the light and left that detested anarchist den.

Student: Detested? Really?

Director: What sort of reputation does anarchy have now?

Student: One of the worst reputations there is.

Director: Do you think that will suddenly change?

Student: If they see our success? Yes.

Director: Alright. Maybe the den won't be detested. But it will be seen as a fool's paradise.

Student: Yes, I agree with that. Paradise is always for 'fools'. But I'd rather be foolish in this way. So you really think relocation will work?

Director: Why not? It will be expensive, but worth it.

Student: Why will it be expensive?

Director: Because we want to make it attractive.

Student: But not that attractive.

Director: What fool would trade in a happy life?

Student: You're right. No one who appreciates life-without-rule would be tempted by this offer. If you're tempted, you are, by definition, one of them.

64

Father: Your contempt for them will backfire on you.

Student: It's not contempt. It's just a low opinion.

Father: Well, that's the thing. No one wants to be low—even with people they're no longer around. A strong spirit might scoff at relocation, dig in, and try to make a point.

Student: Director, do you agree this might happen?

Director: I do. And if they succeed, they are the ruin of life-without-rule.

Student: Why?

Father: I'll tell you why. Because their mad ambition is to be the ruler of life-without-rule. And if that happens, well—you know what that means.

Student: Why are people so horrible? We need to make provisions for this.

Father: What can you do? Whatever provisions you make will only drive the ambition deeper underground.

Director: And that's attractive to some.

Student: What do you mean?

Director: The underground can be an enigma that makes people wonder.

Student: Wonder what?

Director: If there's something more they don't see.

Student: And this makes them wonder if there's more to life than what they live?

Director: Yes. And this underground soul will see this in them. And he will play on this wonder. He will play it right into rule.

Father: I believe it. Anarchists are just that naive.

Student: But it's a beautiful naiveté!

Director: It is. But it's a weakness, nonetheless.

Student: We have to root the underground out.

Father: What will you have? A secret police?

Student: Of course not. We'll simply not leave them alone.

Director: You'll chide them?

Student: That's exactly what we'll do. We'll force them, gently, to truly be one of us or leave.

Father: How will you know if someone has gone underground?

Student: There will be a certain reserve.

Father: So no one can be reserved in life-without-rule?

Student: Happy people aren't reserved.

Father: How do you know? Have you ever been reserved?

Student: I have.

Father: Under my very nose?

Student: I learned reserve at school.

Father: I'd say you learned many things at school, reserve not being one.

Student: You see me here, not there.

Director: Are you planning to rule the school?

Student: Ha, ha. Of course not.

Director: So there can be reserve without desire to rule.

Student: Yes.

Director: Maybe there will be those who are reserved in life-without-rule who aren't really a threat.

Student: True.

Director: So how will you know who the trouble makers are?

Student: They'll find quiet ways to agitate for rule. And when they do, we'll sniff them out and shut them down.

Father: And if they're more quiet than you can hear?

Student: Then we'll trust our eyes.

65

Director: What if few can see the trouble brewing?

Student: We'll have to persuade the others.

Director: So persuasion is of vital importance in life-without-rule.

Student: No doubt.

Director: Can we train people in persuasion?

Student: There's no need. They just have to speak from the heart.

Father: Your underground rogues won't speak from their hearts in their quest to rule. And they might be very persuasive indeed.

Director: I think your father has a point.

Student: So what can we do?

Director: Maybe philosophy can help.

Student: How?

Director: Your rogues want people to believe in them. Philosophy challenges belief.

Student: We must question the rogues.

Director: Yes. Question them as though life itself is at stake—because it is.

Student: So we train ourselves in philosophy as a sort of self-defense?

Director: That's an interesting question. I've never thought of philosophy as self-defense. Maybe it is.

Student: Of course it is! If it can see the rogues for what they are? Yes.

Father: What happens when you see them as they are? Do you force them out?

Student: That's hard if many are charmed by them. So philosophy must break the spell.

Father: And if it can't? Do you override the wishes of your peers?

Student: Maybe everyone needs to be a philosopher here. Director, how do we do that?

Director: Through constant training.

Student: We need a culture of philosophy, don't we?

Director: While it's hard to see how that would hurt....

Student: You have doubts?

Director: Culture and philosophy are two different things. Philosophy needs to exist without a culture of philosophy to support it. Philosophy must stand on its own.

Student: Why?

Director: Because leaning on other things is a sort of corruption.

Father: Even I can see that.

Student: What does a corrupt philosophy do?

Director: It fails to question as though life is at stake.

Father: It's not aggressive enough.

Director: Yes, but I have to caution that philosophy proper is also very gentle.

Father: Why be gentle with a rogue?

Director: Even a rogue can harbor important truth. Do we expect them to share freely if we're rough?

Student: You have a point. But are philosophers the only ones who can see this truth?

Director: No. If things are done right, everyone can see. But philosophers do have an advantage. Skill in questioning aids the understanding. So while everyone can see the truth, philosophers might be better able to see what it means.

66

Father: What is philosophy?

Student: It's love of wisdom.

Father: Who will be wise in life-without-rule? Everyone or no one?

Student: We'll each be wise in our own way.

Father: So philosophy must love life-without-rule. Director?

Director: It remains to be seen.

Student: Would you be willing to make the experiment?

Director: I'm not sure I'd be willing to go to Mars. But would I visit a state of anarchy to see what it's like? Yes.

Student: One visit and you'll be hooked!

Director: That would be very nice.

Student: Oh, don't be so tempered in your enthusiasm.

Father: But that's exactly what you need.

Student: What do you mean?

Father: Blinded by enthusiasm, Director will do you no good. You want him to see the full truth about your way of life. How else will this truth spread?

Student: And by 'full truth' you mean good and ugly both.

Father: Of course.

Student: Well, you have a point. The only way we can fix the ugly is if we're aware. Director might make us aware. Will you come and see?

Father: Me? Why not? But I don't think I'll live to see life-without-rule in play.

Student: You never know. Stranger things have happened.

Father: I don't think anything is stranger than your happy state of anarchy. I wish you luck.

Student: If you come to visit, I think you might stay.

Father: Okay, but save a relocation package for me. And you should save one for Director, too. We might be enchanted only for a while.

Student: Why only for a while?

Father: Life might get too boring.

Student: What could be boring about living in a happy state?

Father: I'm used to living my life the way it is. I don't think I could take the change—assuming your life-without-rule can work! Director?

Director: I'm just getting used to my life despite my years. But I'm open to a change.

Student: Good!

Father: You act as though your little anarchy already exists.

Student: It does—wherever like-minded people gather. Little pockets of anarchy here and there. We just have to connect them all.

Director: Do you think the communication revolution favors life-without-rule?

Student: I do. Don't you?

Director: I don't know. There's still a lot of rule. I'm not seeing too much improvement here. And just look who we elect.

Student: Do you think we should be electing anarchists?

Father: Ha! What would they do? Dissolve the government as their first act?

Student: They would run on the promise of making government smaller... and smaller... and smaller. That could work, couldn't it?

Director: Over time? Yes. But it doesn't address the problem of societal rule. We might shrink the state and embolden and empower society.

Father: What's this? Do anarchists want to do away with society?

Student: If it's based on the general will? Of course.

Father: How can we tell if it's based on the general will?

Student: There will be the kind of distortions we described.

Father: But can't people have distortions without the general will?

Student: Not really, barring mental illness and the like.

Father: So most everyone in a state of anarchy will see things for what they are.

Student: That's the main reason to be in this state.

Director: I thought the main reason was happiness.

Student: Well, yes. But clear sight lends itself to happiness.

Director: Maybe. But there have been studies showing that depressed people see things more clearly than happy people.

Student: What sort of studies?

Director: Scientific studies.

Student: What do you mean by 'more clearly'?

Director: The subjects were presented with different scenarios and then were asked to describe those scenarios. The mildly depressed people scored consistently higher than the happy people. They described things more as they are.

Student: Oh who's to say who's happy or depressed?

Father: If you can't tell the difference between happy and depressed, I'm not sure you're seeing things very clearly, Son.

Student: Okay. But, Director, why do you think the depressed score better?

Director: Maybe they have separated, at least in part, from the general will; and so they can see a little better. But the pressure of the general will tells with time. It leads them to feel depressed.

67

Student: Societal rule can do this to you.

Father: Give us an example of societal rule.

Student: It often has to do with money. Money rules.

Father: I thought you said money is just a facilitator, or something like that.

Student: In an anarchy, yes. But before? It's rule.

Director: What is money?

Student: Belief in its value. Coins, paper, bits of leather, whatever—the value comes through the belief that it's valuable.

Director: That may be the greatest belief there is today.

Father: You have a point. I look at my accounts on my computer and I believe I see value. When the numbers on the screen go up, I'm happy; when they go down, I'm down. All from numbers I believe in on a screen.

Director: Would you undermine belief in money, Student?

Student: I would.

Director: How?

Student: I... don't know. It's a deeply entrenched belief.

Director: Well, it's a start to point out that fact. Maybe others will come along and help us here.

Father: Director, why are you saying 'us'?

Director: Student is saying interesting things. I'd like to see where they go.

Father: But do you know what you're saying? Do you have any idea what happens when belief in money dies? You have panic. You have a free falling economy. You have Germany between the wars. Inflation out of control. Is that really what you want?

Student: Of course that's not what we want. Director, tell him what we want.

Director: We want people to stop believing in money—and start knowing what it is.

Father: Now you're talking sense. The better people know money, the better off they'll be.

Student: I agree. But I have a feeling we differ on how they'll be better off.

Director: What's your idea?

Student: That their care for money will wither away.

Director: And your idea, Father?

Father: That they'll learn the value of a dollar.

Director: What is the value of a dollar?

Father: A dollar rules us so much while we earn, and allows us to rule so much once we possess.

Student: I'm surprised you admit as much.

Father: Why shouldn't I? Money is all about rule. The value of a dollar is the extent of its rule.

Director: So those who earn great amounts of money are ruled a great deal?

Father: Yes, of course. And once they have it, they are enabled to rule others.

Director: Student, this sounds like a bigger challenge than even the general will.

Student: Yes. So it seems we do have to do away with money somehow. We don't want a great big crash. We have to ease into it.

Director: How?

Student: We start by teaching people the truth about money—be ruled, then rule. A lot of people will feel that being ruled is no good.

Director: What kind of person feels being ruled is good?

Student: The kind dying to get to the second part.

Director: The longing for money involves the lust to rule.

Student: Yes, to put it simply.

Director: Can we say why a person might lust to rule?

Student: Who can say? It's probably a function of the general will, but this time as part of the economy.

Director: Does it go like this? Many people agree that money is the greatest good, and a sort of general will forms up around the idea, and this distorts the soul?

Student: Exactly.

Director: Father, you've earned lots of money in your life—though less than your father did. Does what we're saying make sense?

Father: It does. But I don't think a desire to rule is bad. Someone has to rule. And who better than someone who's tasted the other side?

68

Director: Why isn't desire to rule bad?

Father: Because rule is necessary—or so says the whole known history of the world.

Director: Would you say it's a necessary evil, or would you say it's a positive good?

Father: I think it's a necessary evil.

Director: Why is it necessary?

Father: Because most people can't be trusted when left to their own devices.

Director: Student, you trust most people, don't you?

Student: Under the right circumstances, I trust all people.

Father: And that makes all the difference here. Even under optimal conditions, I would trust very few.

Director: How does rule help?

Father: When you rule someone, you keep them in check.

Director: They can't do the bad things they would otherwise do.

Father: That's right.

Director: Is it fun to keep someone in check?

Father: Fun? Ha! No, it's work.

Director: The work isn't pleasant?

Father: The work is satisfying.

Director: Ah. That's why people long for this work.

Father: There's nothing greater in life than satisfaction.

Director: Tell us. Does satisfaction have something in common with revenge?

Father: There's some truth in that.

Student: Revenge for what?

Father: While you're earning, people can make it very difficult for you—the bad sort of people. They rule you hard.

Director: And when it's your turn to rule, you take revenge. What kind of revenge?

Father: I rule them hard right back.

Director: But can you always rule the people who were hard on you? The exact same people?

Father: No, that's rare. But you know the type. And so you rule the type.

Director: That introduces a certain amount of generalness, doesn't it?

Father: I suppose it does. But there's no other way.

Student: Of course there is! Put up with the rule while you earn, but then set yourself free! Then when the next generation of earners comes along, they'll be free while they earn—because people like you will leave them alone! And then they'll have no desire for revenge. Break the chain, Father. Break the chain.

Director: So money doesn't have to be about rule.

Father: In theory, this all sounds fine. In practice? We're in utopia again. The desire to rule is in nearly every human heart.

Director: And this is reflected in the general will?

Father: It's what makes the general will what it is. But the general will limits the individual desire. It's the lesser of two evils.

Student: I'm wary of these 'lesser of two evils' arguments. They can be used to justify anything. I don't believe rule is a natural desire. To the extent it's there, it's because of the general will.

69

Director: Where does the general will come from?

Student: From a longing to resist coupled with hope.

Father: You can't really think that.

Director: Student, can you say more?

Student: It was born in times of tyranny. There was a secret yearning for freedom. People wished for another sort of rule, any sort of rule. So long as the tyrant was replaced, no one cared if it were by a king, an aristocracy, or a democracy. They simply longed for change.

Father: How does a general will form from that?

Student: How doesn't a general will form from that? Think of all those people sharing their greatest desire! That's the crucible in which the general will was forged.

Director: So this will was then directed toward overthrowing the tyrant and creating a new form of rule.

Student: Exactly.

Director: But let me guess. The general will didn't step down once the work was done.

Student: You know how it goes. The work is never really done.

Director: So the general will became a fact of a daily life.

Student: Yes, until it reached its greatest height under democracy today.

Director: Why didn't it reach its height under previous democracies?

Student: They were too unstable. We learned from their mistakes and created modern democracy, a tempered democracy. But we are fast outgrowing our form.

Director: What does that mean? The general will is no longer of use?

Student: It's harmful. And it's always been harmful, in a way. But, as my father would say, it was the lesser of two evils—tyranny or general will. I'd take the latter any day.

Director: Is tyranny ever the lesser of two evils?

Student: If it is, we're talking about truly terrible times.

Father: Tyranny is the easy way out of terrible times. It happens when the will of the people breaks.

Director: What if it's not broken? What if the people just surrender their will?

Father: Tyranny results.

Student: There can be no tyranny if no one goes along. Surrender of the general will is the beginning of life-without-rule. And no one living this life would ever invite a tyrant in.

Father: In your perfect world, no—no one would. I find it hard to argue with you.

Student: What do you mean? You agree?

Father: No. What I mean is this. I say people are bad; you say people are good. Everything follows from this. We can't agree

Director: Is it fair to say some will be good and some will be bad?

Father: I think it is.

Student: It isn't fair—because it isn't true.

Father: The ones you banish aren't bad?

Student: Well....

Father: Ha!

Director: Regardless of whether people are good or bad, can't they be taught?

Father: What do you think, Student? Will you take over the education of all the children to make them good?

Student: I will provide them with an environment that will allow them to thrive.

Father: I don't think you'll ever have the chance to create that environment.

Student: Why not?

Father: Unless you go to Mars, you need a time and place where rule is lax. That's how you'll have the space you need. But this place is far from lax in rule.

Director: You're saying there's still virtue in the regime.

Father: Virtue, yes. A great amount.

Student: What are you two talking about? Virtue? Are you equating virtue with rule?

Father: Rule is the virtue of all regimes.

Student: Does virtue mean strength?

Father: Strength, vigor, policy. Think of it in Machiavelli's sense concerning ancient republican Rome.

Student: Well, people do compare us with them—but more often with imperial Rome.

Father: Forget about Rome. This country is strong. And it has no need of your education.

Director: Why not?

Father: If we educate the children in life-without-rule, we'll make it weak. Do you deny it, Student? Your happy life is one of anarchy. Yes?

Student: Yes.

Father: Anarchy is the sworn enemy of all regimes. No?

Student: Well....

Father: Oh, of course it is. Everyone knows that. And you think you can undermine the regime by teaching its youth, teaching against the regime. You're suddenly quiet.

Director: He's realizing the magnitude of his task.

Father: Yes, and others will realize what he's about and seek to rip out the weed before it grows.

70

Director: He'll be forced to cloak what he does.

Father: He will. And secrecy will undermine the purity of his cause. Once you're secret with one thing, why not be secret in more?

Director: But let's suppose he's only secret in the one, the undermining of the regime. How will the students come to understand? What if they imagine anything but that?

Father: They'll be idealists who don't know the truth before their very eyes.

Director: So Student will have to initiate them, at some point, into the mysteries.

Father: And the minute he does that there's a conspiracy against the government. The authorities will swoop down on them with a vengeance.

Student: Why haven't they swooped down on my class at school?

Father: Because your professor is merely questioning democracy. He's not calling for an actual overthrow of the regime.

Student: What if I just keep up the questioning?

Father: You never take the next step? Nothing will happen. After your friends all graduate from school, what will they do? Most of them will join the ruling class. What will you do?

Student: I'll get an advanced degree and teach. I'll keep up the questioning. I'll carry the torch.

Father: That's fine—so long as you don't start any fires. But you'll be in a funny place.

Student: What do you mean?

Father: You'll criticize our democracy while enjoying its benefits. You'll be ungrateful, to call it what it is.

Student: I'm not ungrateful. But what should I be grateful for? The general will?

Father: I thought you said it shook off tyranny.

Student: That was then; this is now. With tyranny gone—you do agree it's gone?—what need is there for a general will? Why be grateful for something I don't need?

Father: I suspect you don't know what you need.

Student: And you do?

Father: I have a little more experience in life than you do, Son.

Student: Maybe you have the wrong sort of experience.

Director: What's the right experience? None of us has ever experienced anarchy, except for maybe a little touch here and there.

Student: I get this touch in class. There are times when no one rules.

Director: The conditions of that very limited anarchy are special, no?

Student: They are. I want to take up teaching in a special setting like that, and create little moments of anarchy—as many as I can.

Director: Because you believe if you do that, eventually, good results will follow.

Student: I do believe that—with all my heart.

71

Director: Hmm.

Student: What is it?

Director: How do you know bad results won't follow?

Student: What do you mean?

Director: What if there are students who go off and decide no one is going to rule them, and they grant themselves license to commit all sorts of crimes.

Student: No, those won't be the kinds of students I'll have.

Director: How do you know?

Student: I'll know because... because... I'll be teaching at a good university.

Father: Ha, ha. As if some of the worst criminals don't come from good schools.

Director: Your father has a point. So what if you spend your life teaching, and some go off and do good things, and some go off and do bad things—would you be happy with that?

Student: No.

Director: You would only be happy if everyone goes off and does good things?

Student: Yes.

Father: You're in for a lot of unhappiness then.

Director: Tell us, Student. Would you be unhappy because you believe that a taste of anarchy should be enough to motivate anyone to strive for more, strive in a good way?

Student: Yes. The taste should awaken them to what's possible in life. Once tasted, no one is satisfied with anything less.

Director: Father, have you tasted anarchy?

Father: I have. In war.

Director: Does nothing else satisfy quite like that?

Father: The opposite.

Director: Student, does this challenge your belief?

Student: Look, I'm not trying to question my father's experience of war. Maybe we have to make an exception for the anarchy of war. In fact, maybe that's why anarchy has a bad name.

Director: Because most experience it in the throes of war?

Student: Yes. And I think my father has been remarkably patient with me today, given his feelings about anarchy.

Father: I'm open to the possibility that there's more to it than what I know. But many people aren't going to be patient with you. In fact, they'll react violently toward you. I don't want that. So teach; be a radical, even. But follow the rules.

Director: One of the rules is that professors lead the class.

Student: I won't agree to follow that rule. Sometimes the students should lead.

Director: Will you grade your students?

Student: The class I'm in now is pass or fail.

Director: How do you pass?

Student: By showing up and contributing to the discussion.

Director: What if you contribute by saying, 'I think you're all crazy and I won't take part'?

Student: That would be enough. Sometimes the most one can do is listen.

Father: What will you do with parents who come to you and say you're wasting their money?

Student: I don't think they'll come to me very often. They'll go to their children. And that's the first test.

Director: Of what?

Student: What the students have learned.

Father: About what?

Student: The rule that parents exercise over their children.

Father: If they're paying for school the parents have rights. Will you teach your students to take out loans so the parents don't pay and therefore have no say?

Student: I think that's a good idea.

Father: But those loans will rule over the students a good long while. So it's either the rule of the parents or the rule of the bank.

Student: Then I'll have to teach where there is no tuition, or very little.

Father: Then you'll be teaching at a place that doesn't pay, or pays very little.

Student: I don't need much.

Father: I should have made you work before sending you to school.

Student: So I could learn the value of a dollar.

Father: Yes.

72

Director: So let's be clear. Government rules. Society rules. Money rules. Teachers rule. Parents rule. And all of these overlap to some degree. But are we leaving anything out?

Father: The rule of owners over pets.

Student: Be serious.

Father: I am! Don't you think owners rule their pets?

Student: First of all, they're parents, not owners. Second, with any good parent it's the opposite—the animal rules them. I see that with your little dog every day.

Father: Ha, ha. You've got me. But still, I do rule. I control the animal's life. Fortunately, I happen to be a good parent. Many aren't; their rule is very bad. But my point is this. Will we have anarchy when it comes to dogs and cats? I can't think you'd want this.

Student: But I do. Rule harms the parents. And yes, there is benevolent rule, which is better for both animal and human. But I compare that to democracy—the best of the various evils. The problem has to do with what you said when you called the humans owners. No one can own another living creature. Creatures are by nature free.

Father: So in anarchy there are no pets?

Student: None.

Father: What kind of anarchic dictator are you?

Student: Humans' relationship with animals will be better than ever before. There will be true friendship. If an animal wants to take up living with certain humans, it will do so freely. If it wants to leave after a while, so be it.

Director: Tell us, Student. Do anarchists eat meat?

Student: Of course not. There's tyranny in meat.

Father: And what about the poor potatoes and apples and grains of wheat? Don't we tyrannize over them?

Student: If you can't tell the difference between a pig and an apple I can't help you, Dad.

Director: Is the relationship you'd have us have with animals a model for our relationships with humans?

Student: I think it's a good model, yes. Like I said, there will be no marriages.

Director: What about families?

Student: Not in the sense we know them today.

Father: If not in that sense, who will take the time and trouble and expense to raise a child?

Student: People who love children.

Director: So you're not necessarily raising your own child.

Student: Not necessarily. We do this today with adoptions and foster care.

Father: Yes, but those are the exceptions.

Student: And maybe they will be still. I don't know. My point is that people won't be forced. They will have options.

Father: The more you talk, the further away life-without-rule seems. You really do mean it, don't you?

Student: Mean what?

Father: That there will be no rules. Or can anarchists agree to certain rules?

Student: Why would they?

Father: So they can live with one another!

Student: The only sense in which we might say there's a rule, is our deference to human nature.

Father: Well, that's where it all falls apart. Humans are not what you think they are.

Student: I'm open to being wrong.

Director: What will you do if you find yourself in life-without-rule, but things are going wrong?

Student: Wrong like there's still rule?

Director: No, I mean even without rule people are fighting, and so on. What would you do?

Student: I don't think that would happen.

Director: But if it did?

Student: If? Someone would have to take charge of the situation.

Director: Someone would have to rule.

Father: The executive.

Student: But maybe he or she can persuade instead of rule.

Father: The only persuasion some people know comes through the mouth of a gun. So what if you find people like that?

Student: I won't. But if I did....

Father: You'd take aim?

Student: Maybe. But I wouldn't want to rule with the gun. I'd banish them instead.

73

Father: Ah, having to exercise banishment again. Doesn't that shake your confidence?

Student: No, because I'm inspired by those who'll remain. And you can tell me that in six months the same trouble will arise. I say it won't. At some point we just have to put it to the test.

Father: But the conditions of a successful test are so far away you'll never have the chance.

Director: Student, can a way of life be good, in a very real and practical way, if it can never be reached?

Student: We'll just try a colony. If not on Mars, then somewhere here.

Director: What would it take?

Student: Enough money to set us up.

Director: And then you pull the ladder up behind you?

Student: Yes.

Father: But not strictly speaking.

Student: Yes, strictly speaking. We don't want contamination from the rule-infected world.

Father: But then you can't share your success.

Student: That's... true. But success has ruined more than one experiment.

Director: So what can you do?

Student: Maybe after many years of success, we'll send one of the colony's elders back to report on our affairs.

Director: What will happen then?

Father: I'll tell you what will happen then. Your colony will be overwhelmed.

Director: He has a point. People love a success.

Student: Then let them set up their own colonies and leave ours alone.

Father: I thought you trust in human nature. Why not trust the humans who thrill at your success?

Student: We can only take on so many. Most won't be ready for what life-without-rule entails.

Father: But, you know, those who don't thrill will think there's something wrong with you, to live the way you do. And then they'll attack.

Student: I don't doubt that's true. So we must isolate ourselves.

Father: But it will never work. Pull the ladder up after you, as you may—someone will know where you've gone. Eventually you'll be found.

Student: But maybe there's natural selection here. Who will go to the trouble to find us but those with an interest in life-without-rule?

Father: Who? Reporters, for one. What a great story they'd have. 'Anarchist Colony Breaks Away from the World.'

Student: Why can't people just leave each other alone?

Father: I don't know why. But if you want to be left alone you have to fight.

Student: So we fight the reporters who come? What does that mean? We kill them?

Father: Oh, I'm not saying that. Though you may have to put them in jail.

Student: No, what kind of example would that set? I don't want any prisoners marring our life.

Father: Well, there are only two choices—keep them or send them away.

Student: We'll send them away—before they've seen anything of us.

Father: So you'll need guards?

Student: No, no guards. That smacks of rule.

Father: How will you intercept them before they've seen anything?

Student: All of us will agree that if any outsiders come, we'll raise an alarm—and then the community will decide whether to usher them out.

Father: That will only intrigue people and make things worse.

74

Student: Then it will have to be isolation.

Father: Chaos in isolation. Great.

Student: I've told you it won't be chaos. Life-without-rule will be better organized than life-under-rule.

Director: Why?

Student: Because we'll be organized according to nature. All the pieces will fit together when needed. No one will have to be coerced. We'll all know what needs to be done.

Director: How do you know all the pieces will fit so well?

Student: Humans are flexible when they're not locked into place by rule. They fit to one another well and bond under pressure.

Father: But that bonding is the beginning of rule.

Student: How so?

Father: One group bonds here; another bonds there. Each wants to stick together and rule the other.

Student: No. When different groups meet they'll only want to form new bonds.

Father: This easy bonding won't stand in the face of danger.

Student: Why not?

Father: Because fear will overcome the bond.

Student: Fear will reinforce the bond.

Director: And when the bond is strengthened?

Student: All will know what needs to be done.

Father: By miracle, of course.

Student: They'll know through common interest. The danger they face is rule. Those who live life-without-rule can sense it a mile away. They'll coordinate their resistance.

Director: What language will they speak?

Student: What?

Director: What language? Or won't they have a common language?

Student: They might... not.

Father: How would they communicate in time of danger?

Student: There will be interpreters.

Father: That slows things down and allows for misunderstandings.

Student: Misunderstandings occur even when people speak the same language.

Director: Student, would you have all those who live life-without-rule speaking a common tongue if you could?

Student: No.

Director: Why not?

Student: Because language is a form of rule.

Father: Oh, you're taking it too far!

Student: Tell me. How do we think?

Father: We just... think!

Student: Yes, but what do we use to think?

Father: Our brains.

Student: Sure. Also our hearts. But what do we use? Words. If words are imposed, thought is imposed.

Director: I think he has a point.

Student: Learning a language helps free the mind. Our people in life-without-rule will naturally wish to keep their minds free. And so they'll learn many other tongues. Communication won't be as difficult as you might think.

75

Director: What about the languages of the arts?

Student: We will positively thrive when it comes to this.

Director: Why?

Student: Because with free minds so much creativity is possible!

Director: In the written arts?

Student: And the spoken arts, yes.

Director: Does it go without saying that music will thrive?

Student: Music will thrive. But people will have to learn this language, too. Musicians will be free from conventions and make original music, like nothing anyone has ever heard.

Director: And the visual arts? Painting, for instance?

Student: The same as music—very free painters making wonderful things.

Director: These arts will speak straight to the heart?

Student: Yes.

Director: Is there a danger that this sort of art can be a form of rule, rule over the heart? After all, language can be a sort of rule.

Student: I know what you mean. I'll have to think about this more. But for now I want to say no.

Director: Perhaps these arts can be the greatest export from life-without-rule.

Student: That's a good point. This art can build bridges. And where there are bridges there can be hope.

Father: No more isolation when you can hope to conquer the outside world?

Student: Not conquer, but show them what's possible here.

Director: A very free life.

Student: Yes, a very free life.

Father: But a very poor life.

Student: People will have what they need.

Father: Some will need to work the fields all day while some stay home to write and compose?

Student: Maybe. But what's more likely is that all will 'work the fields'—whatever that means—and some will write and compose at night.

Director: Will there be fame?

Student: Not in the sense we have it now.

Director: Why not?

Student: In life-under-rule, people are looking for escape. Artists, of whatever sort, are eager to provide that for them. In life-without-rule, no one is looking to escape. There is nothing to escape. So art is not escapist. Art enhances the good life they already live. So people love art, but for different reasons. Therefore, they praise the artist but never worship her or him.

Father: But artists can become well known. Right?

Student: True. But renown and fame can be very different things.

Director: Have you ever heard that people are trapped by their fame?

Student: And they are. But no one is ever trapped by renown, properly understood.

Director: What traps the famous?

Student: People expecting too much.

Director: They expect constant escape?

Student: They do. And they expect the famous to be... perfect.

Director: Why do they expect that?

Student: Because escape makes them think good things.

Director: If the famous are good—perfect—does it follow that people will want to be like them?

Student: Of course. But not those in life-without-rule.

Director: Why not?

Student: Those with natural talent might wish to learn from them. But to be like them? No—because they want to stay free.

76

Director: We can learn without being slavish in imitation.

Student: And without having an unhealthy desire to match or surpass the other, yes.

Father: Why is that unhealthy? Haven't you ever heard of healthy competition?

Student: The health is in learning your craft, not measuring yourself against another.

Father: What's wrong with that? Should we pretend others don't exist?

Student: No, we shouldn't pretend.

Director: Should we pretend we're not interested in fame if we are?

Student: No. The only way to rid yourself of that desire is to bring it into the light.

Director: And if it endures despite the light?

Student: Then you know you're not in life-without-rule.

Director: In life-under-rule, is there a secret to fame?

Father: Just create great work and you'll have it.

Student: It doesn't work that way. Many create great work and don't have fame. They stay behind the scenes. Fame is something more.

Director: Fame is a sort of rule? You rule the hearts and minds of your fans?

Student: That's right.

Father: Nonsense. Fame lacks power. Power is something more.

Student: Many of the famous in life-under-rule have power. And do you know why? Many fans lead desperate lives. And in their desperation, they grant power over themselves.

Father: Desperation? Hardly.

Student: But don't you ever ask why they love their artists so? It's all about escape.

Director: And no one wants to escape life-without-rule.

Student: They really don't. In fact, those in the outer world want to escape to life-without-rule.

Father: You really think that's what they want?

Student: Desperately, yes.

Father: But they don't want your life-without-rule. They want no rules—on their own terms. They want their current life, but with no rules.

Student: They don't know what they want.

Director: We all want the same thing?

Student: To the extent we're all human we do.

Director: Some of us aren't human?

Student: Rule can distort someone so badly that they're no longer human. Think of vicious tyrants. Think of any of the wildly corrupt.

Director: And just to be clear, rule corrupts... why?

Student: Because humans aren't meant to rule or be ruled.

Director: You're saying there's a third way.

Student: Yes, and it's the only true way.

Father: Sure. But all you've done today is assert this is true. I could assert the opposite, and all of history is on my side.

Student: History is a tale told by the winners. You've heard that.

Father: I have.

Student: Sometimes it's a tale told by the losers.

Father: I haven't heard that.

Student: My point is that win or lose, ruler or ruled, it's all the same. It's all about rule. History deals in rule. There is no history of life-without-rule.

77

Father: People won't want to preserve the memory of glorious deeds?

Student: First of all, there will be no glorious deeds. Second, for deeds worth remembering, the people involved will remember. And that's enough.

Father: People won't want to know what, for instance, their great-grandparents did before they were born?

Student: What need is there for that?

Father: It's only... natural!

Student: It's a form of rule.

Father: Oh, stop it. What rule is there in that?

Student: The rule of the past over the present. The younger generation will imagine these things as something to live up to.

Father: What's wrong with that?

Student: It fetters the mind. The youths should be free to do what suits their nature, not shackle themselves to deeds from the past.

Father: There is no striving toward greatness in life-without-rule, is there?

Student: None.

Father: What kind of a world is it with no greatness?

Student: A peaceful world full of love.

Father: Ha!

Director: Is it the peace or the love you find laughable, Father?

Father: It's the naive faith that these things are enough to prevail.

Director: Prevail over what, rule?

Father: Prevail over life's many difficulties. Look, I'm in favor of peace and love. But life takes more than that. Striving toward greatness helps.

Director: How?

Father: It creates a sort of slipstream in which others can follow. This means the great one opens the way. No one is opening any ways in life-without-rule.

Student: That's because the ways are already open.

Father: What you really mean is that you'll be free to go... nowhere.

Student: What does it mean to go somewhere in life? That's what you want, right?

Father: That's what I want for you. And what does it mean? It means to achieve. Fortune and fame, sure. But it can simply mean winning the respect and admiration of your peers.

Student: But we'll have admiration and respect in life-without-rule!

Father: Respect and admiration of all for all.

Student: What's wrong with that?

Father: If everyone is admired, no one is admired.

Student: That's false logic. True logic says that if everyone is admired, everyone is admired. Admiration isn't cheapened by many being admired. That's like saying if everyone is treated well, no one is treated well. Yours is the logic of rule.

Director: Can you say more?

Student: Rule believes that you must rule or be ruled. Under this way of looking at things, if everyone rules no one rules. There must be those who are ruled. And so rulers strive to be among the few who rule. They strive to be ever fewer, ever more elite. The ultimate in rule is the rule of one. Democracy is least favored by those who would rule because of reasons I'm sure you understand.

Director: So in democracies there are levels of rule.

Student: Yes, exactly. Those who would rule, who lust after rule, create cliques of rule above the rule of the many. But the irony here is that they must tailor their rule to suit the many. They are above the many and servants of the many at once. Democracy, to them, has a bad taste.

78

Director: And so they stress that we don't live in a democracy. We live in a republic.

Student: Republican democracy is how they like to phrase it. It's direct democracy's opposite.

Father: And direct democracy is as close to anarchy is it gets.

Student: But for the general will.

Father: Would you prefer something else? A monarchy?

Student: I sometimes think yes. The transition to life-without-rule might be smoother in a monarchy.

Director: How so?

Student: A monarch who believes in life-without-rule could educate her or his people that way.

Father: And do what? Resign?

Student: Eventually, yes. But much would have to be worked out before.

Father: I'm glad you admit that. But these things will never be worked out.

Student: Why not?

Father: Monarchs have people who surround them. The monarch would have to educate them first. But these people believe in rule with all their hearts, more so than your monarch does.

Student: That's true.

Father: So what do you do about them?

Student: The monarch could disenfranchise them, strip them of whatever power they have.

Father: And then they'll be happy in life-without-rule?

Student: Well, no. The monarch might have to send them away.

Father: Send any with power or influence away?

Student: Yes. And then set the people free.

Father: The monarch would just be one of them.

Student: And it would be the greatest delight of her or his life.

Father: Director, what do you think?

Director: Student has a point. Transition from monarchy might be easier. In democracy, many have relatively small amounts of power. It's not concentrated as in a monarchy. And yet they love their power just the same. Can we send so many power loving democrats away? It can hardly be done.

Father: So what are we saying? That if we democrats want life-without-rule, we need to concentrate power—then throw it all away?

Student: In so many words? Yes.

Father: That's a dangerous game. You really think you'll get your king or queen to resign?

Student: It's easier to persuade one woman or man than many petty chiefs. Yes, it takes some luck. But the odds are better this way. Besides, everyone—or almost everyone—knows that ultimate power is out of reach. This tempers their ambitions, making persuasion toward life-without-rule a possibility, if not a likelihood.

Father: Anarchists in favor of monarchy. Who would have guessed? What about aristocracy? A distant second best?

Student: Yes. It's easier to persuade few than many.

Father: But if one of the few steps down, another will take their place. You'd have to get them to all step down at once. And that will never happen.

79

Director: When one steps down, why are we sure another will take their place?

Father: Because everyone is endlessly striving for place.

Director: Everyone?

Father: Well, the aristocrats.

Director: And in a democracy?

Father: Everyone strives.

Director: Is striving a virtue?

Father: It can be.

Director: How?

Father: It brings out your best. But, Son, I'm afraid you wouldn't know about this.

Student: Oh? Why not?

Father: Because in life-without-rule, no one will strive.

Student: What makes you say that?

Father: Laziness will be everyone's god. I mean, what are your people going to do but laze about?

Student: You're so wrong I don't even know where to begin! Our people will work with a pleasure unknown to those who live life-under-rule. Work will correlate directly with personal success, unlike today. Today, people work for the benefit of shareholders, who do no work at all. People feel this disconnect. Some think that's just the way it is. Some resent.

Father: I'm glad you mentioned that latter thing. Your anarchy is based on resentment. This is a terrible thing on which to start a life.

Student: Resentment isn't the thing. People don't like to resent. They wish they didn't. But resentment stirs thought. And thought, in the end, leads to life-without-rule. Life-without-rule is free of resentment, and any related feelings. The feelings of life-without-rule are clean.

Father: So you pronounce. There's no example of anarchy you can site. So you say whatever you will.

Student: The animal kingdom knows anarchy. Yes, there are predators and prey. But the predators don't rule the prey. The mouse lives a life free, despite the danger from the cat.

Director: Are there predators and prey in human anarchy?

Student: Humans are different than animals in just this. No, there are no predators and prey outside rule.

Father: That's just a guess on your part. How do you know?

Student: Predator animals hunt in order to eat. Humans can farm.

Director: You'll ban hunters from your realm?

Student: The anarchist ideal is the farm.

Father: I like meat.

Student: If you knew animals well, you wouldn't.

Father: Then why do pet lovers across the world love meat?

Student: I... can't answer for them.

Director: But you think they're wrong.

Student: I do.

Father: I know people with pigs as pets who still eat pork. What does that say?

Student: It says they love their own but not the rest.

Director: Should they not love their own?

Student: Of course not.

Director: But you'd have them love the rest, the like.

Student: I would.

Director: Because like is kin, and we should love our kin?

Student: Well....

Father: Why do you have a problem with that? What's wrong with kin?

Student: Some kin are... bad.

Father: And some people say we should love them nonetheless.

Student: I'm not 'some people'.

Father: Neither am I. There's no good reason on Earth to love the bad.

Student: Then why do you love those who would rule?

Father: Because rule isn't bad. In fact, rule is good.

Student: Good? How is it good?

Father: It keeps the bad in check.

Student: Maybe if they weren't held in check they wouldn't be bad.

Father: And maybe the moon is made of cheese.

80

Director: Student, have you heard this saying? 'The strong do what they can, and the weak suffer what they must.'

Student: The Athenians said that to the Melians in the Peloponnesian War. I never liked the Athenians. They killed all the Melian men and enslaved the women and children, you know.

Director: Yes. But what do you think of what they said?

Student: They were speaking of rule, rule of the worst possible sort—the rule of naked force, stripped of notions of justice.

Director: Didn't you say there was no need for justice in life-without-rule?

Student: But that emphatically wasn't life-without-rule.

Director: Prior to life-without-rule there is a need for justice?

Student: Justice can temper rule.

Director: Can?

Student: Justice can also make rule worse.

Director: How?

Student: The belief in the justice of your violent cause amplifies the harm.

Father: But it can also mislead.

Director: How so?

Father: It can make you think you're stronger than you are.

Director: As did the Athenians?

Father: They were funny. They sometimes spoke of naked force and sometimes spoke of justice. All I know is that they believed in themselves, over-reached, and lost the war.

Director: What of the Spartans?

Father: They believed in force.

Director: No justice with them?

Father: They believed justice should guide the use of force.

Student: Whose justice?

Father: Theirs.

Director: Were the Spartans just?

Father: Who cares? They won the war. They won because they had more virtue, more force.

Director: Student?

Student: I think my father is right.

Director: So if a nation of virtue and force comes up against your anarchy....

Student: We'd have to have more virtue and force.

Director: How would you have it?

Student: By nature.

Director: People would be willing to die to protect their life-without-rule?

Student: Yes, their free way of life and those they love. That's all in the world there is to protect.

Director: Live free or die?

Student: That ancient patriot had it exactly right. That was a cry in the wild for life-without-rule. There are greater ills in life than death.

Father: Your fellow anarchists would truly be motivated by that?

Student: Truly.

Father: If so, then I must admit—they are a greater fighting force than I imagined. I would fight for that.

Director: Would you ever fight for rule-or-be-ruled?

Student: No one fights for that.

Director: Really? Isn't that what the Athenians did?

Father: The Spartans fought to live free or die—live free against imperial Athens.

Student: The Spartans at the time had an empire of their own.

Father: Yes—but they didn't brag about it, now did they?

81

Director: So it's best to be quiet about those you rule.

Student: There's something evil about silence in rule.

Director: Better to be brazen like the Athenians?

Student: At least then you know what you're dealing with.

Director: Sparta's slaves, the Helots, they didn't know what they were dealing with?

Student: Of course they knew.

Director: But Greece didn't know?

Student: No, all of Greece knew.

Director: So where is the silent evil?

Student: It's evil that no one said a thing.

Director: Did anyone say anything about Athens' conquest of the Melians?

Student: One of their own said all that needed to be said. Thucydides.

Director: By reporting what must have been said, he said all there was to say?

Student: Yes.

Director: He didn't report on the Spartans?

Student: Well....

Director: Slaves were common in the ancient world.

Student: That doesn't make slavery right. Slavery is the worst sort of rule. The slave lacks basic human rights.

Director: Will there be rights in life-without-rule?

Student: Rights aren't necessary there.

Director: Rights protect those who are subject to potential oppression.

Student: Exactly so. There are no potential oppressors in life-without-rule.

Father: Why not?

Student: Everyone is too busy living their own lives to bother with anyone else.

Father: Are you saying these people are selfish?

Student: Of course they're selfish. They care about themselves and act on that care. But that doesn't mean they don't care for others, too. I know you find all of this hard to believe.

Father: No, I find it impossible to believe. And I'm amazed you believe it. Director, do you believe?

Director: No, I don't. Though I confess to a fascination with Student's belief.

Student: Why don't you believe?

Director: Because I think humans are mixed. So in order to achieve your life-without-rule, you need to select the right humans. Which means you must be very sure in what you know about human nature. What do you know?

Student: I know... know.... I'm not sure.

Director: You just assume because most natures are the same there's nothing to know. Am I right?

Student: Well....

Father: He has you there, Son. The charm of your scheme is that there's nothing to know. It all takes care of itself. Am I right?

Student: I.... But what is there to know?

82

Father: To start with you have to know good nature from bad. You can't just believe there is no good or bad. You have to know them for what they are.

Student: And I suppose you'll tell me I have to trust the good.

Father: Of course. And never trust the bad.

Student: So tell me, Dad, what's a good rule of thumb for whom I should trust?

Father: Trust those with honor.

Director: Is there honor and dishonor in life-without-rule?

Student: I... don't know.

Father: What's this? Something you don't know?

Student: Oh, stop. You two have made your point. I'm listening to you now.

Director: Father, we should explain to Student what honor is.

Father: Honor is faith you put in yourself.

Director: And dishonor?

Father: That's what happens when your deeds violate this faith.

Student: Yes, but what if your deeds in keeping with your faith harm others?

Father: That's what we call bad faith.

Director: Tell us, Student. Do you think being true to yourself differs from having faith in yourself?

Student: I'm not sure. I've never thought about it before.

Father: By 'true', do we mean living up to our every whim, our every desire?

Student: Of course not.

Director: What do we mean by 'living up to'?

Father: Acknowledging these desires as actual fact. I like cotton candy. Do I eat it all the time? No. But I don't deny I like it.

Director: Why don't you eat it all the time?

Father: Because it's nothing more than spun up sugar.

Director: So you rule this desire of yours?

Father: Absolutely. Self-rule is a necessity in this world. Even when I act on my desire, I'm still in full control. I deliberate and decide when to indulge.

Director: How can we best deliberate and decide?

Father: We have to think of the consequences of our choice.

Director: How do we know what the consequences will be?

Father: This is very hard. We can start by listening to our elders. Their experience can teach us much.

Director: I'm sure it can. And is that, ultimately, how we learn? From their experience?

Father: Well, no. I mean, we learn from our experience, too, of course.

Director: Of course. But we can learn from our elders' words because they in turn learned from both experience and words?

Father: Right.

Director: But somewhere way back there in time was the first experience, and there were no elders' words to guide. How do we know the right choice was made?

Father: Maybe it wasn't. But we can learn from mistakes.

Director: And so the elders judged and learned and handed down their wisdom. But, Father, hand-me-down clothes often don't fit.

Student: Exactly. Words of wisdom must be tailored to present tense life.

Father: Life doesn't change as much as you think.

Student: Of course it does. Each life is wholly unique.

Father: Ah, snowflakes again.

Student: There's no denying each of us is unique. Old wisdom never applies.

Father: When we're in a raging blizzard there is no time to contemplate the uniqueness of the flakes.

Director: Tell us something, Father. Must we tailor our thoughts to what comes before us? Or can our thoughts withstand the outside world?

Father: Now that's a serious question.

Student: I'm not sure I understand what's asked.

Father: He wants to know how long we hold fast.

Student: To what we think wise?

Father: Yes. I'll say this. Wisdom is merely a guide, not an absolute.

Student: Of course it's a guide. Wisdom can never be absolute.

Director: Why?

Student: Because wisdom, like justice, is blind.

Director: All wisdom?

Student: All inherited wisdom. It wasn't designed for our needs.

Director: What does it take to meet our needs?

Student: Courage.

Father: Courage, sure. But discipline, and better yet—will.

Director: What good is will if we have the wrong thoughts?

Student: It's no good at all.

Director: So we must always begin with our thoughts.

Student: You know, it's funny. That's so obvious it feel like it should go without saying. But I think some people start with will and bend their thoughts toward that.

Father: Like a bow.

Student: You give them too much credit.

Director: Student, you didn't start with your thoughts here today. Did you?

Student: What do you mean?

Director: You took a desire—to live without rule—and let your imagination run wild, never giving thought to what you needed to know.

Student: In other words, I wasn't very wise.

Director: No, you were far from wise. You didn't have an iota of wisdom. But there's something to be said for this.

Student: What?

Director: You were brave.

Student: How do you know that?

Director: You voiced unpopular thoughts. That takes courage—and there is no courage if there's no fear.

Student: What does this have to do with wisdom?

Director: The wise aren't afraid.

83

Father: That's a debatable point.

Student: It doesn't matter one way or another now—because I had something better than wisdom.

Director: What did you have?

Student: Trust.

Director: In your father and me?

Student: Yes.

Director: Trust lessens fear?

Student: Of course.

Director: Does that mean cowards would do well to trust with all their might?

Student: Are you calling me a coward?

Director: Why would you think that?

Student: Because I trust so much in life-without-rule.

Director: Do you believe what you believe because of a fear?

Student: That's what I'm starting to suspect.

Director: Father, we're at a very important point. This could be a watershed moment in Student's life. I don't want to make any mistakes here. Do you have something to say?

Father: Son, I believe your trust in humanity is more the mark of your own good nature than any fear. If you do fear, it's because you want to see yourself in others but you very often don't. That's disconcerting, and might cause fear—in anyone. But you have to conquer this fear. You must know others for what they are. When you know them, you won't be afraid...much.

Director: There, wisdom. What do you think, Student?

Father: No one likes to hear they don't know people for what they are. But I do admit to a certain amount of fear when I encounter others unlike me.

Father: So make a study of them. Learn just what the enemy is. And—

Director: Excuse me. Unlike equates to enemy?

Father: My son is good; others unlike him are bad.

Director: Simply bad?

Father: Bad is bad. Oh, we all have some bad. But those like my son rule themselves. The bad don't have that self-control.

Director: Should we make up for their deficiency?

Student: How?

Director: We rule them, out of an abundance of rule in our own soul. And isn't that always the way?

Student: I don't understand.

Director: There is no outer rule without an overflow of inner rule.

Father: I know what you mean, Director. But tyranny is a type of rule, and there is no self-rule in the tyrant's soul.

Director: Oh, but there is. It's called prudence. Prudence guides all the tyrant's acts.

Student: Even I don't believe that.

Director: How else does a tyrant stay in charge? One false step and he or she is dead.

Student: But tyrants make false steps all the time.

Director: But none that pose a clear threat to their rule. At least that's how it goes with the more successful types.

Father: Let's not talk about successful tyrants.

Director: My point is just that rule begets rule. And if it's true that life is a rule or be ruled affair, we must have as much inner rule as we can.

Student: I think that makes sense—if life is a rule or be ruled affair. And if it is, why wouldn't everyone make inner rule priority number one?

Father: Excuse me for saying, but weren't you just a moment ago longing for life-without-rule? Why wasn't inner rule your priority number one then?

Student: Because life isn't a rule or be ruled affair.

Father: I think it's because you were bent on going against what every sensible person thinks.

Director: Why would he be so bent?

Father: That's what youth does.

Student: That's what philosophers do.

Director: Philosophers do challenge what people think. But they don't often do it through a fantastic belief.

Student: Life-without-rule is a fantastic belief?

Director: Isn't it?

Student: You think I should give it up?

Director: Oh, I don't know. Maybe you need a break. Go off and learn a few things, then return to your belief and see what's to be done.

Father: What's to be done is to forget it for good.

Director: Maybe. But something led Student this way. Don't you think he should find out what it is?

Father: Well, we can't rule ourselves if we don't know ourselves. Son, I don't know what led you here. Director doesn't know what let you here. It's for you to figure out. If you do, you'll know yourself in a way no one else can. And that will make you... unique.

84

Director: And if you don't find out, do you know what you might have?

Student: Tell me.

Director: Anarchy in your soul.

Student: Anarchy in the bad sense.

Director: Yes. Anarchy in the sense of chaos. Who wants chaos in their soul? Do you?

Student: No, I want peace in my soul. That's what everyone wants.

Father: Hot blooded youth doesn't act that way.

Student: Is the blood of age always cold?

Father: It's better when cool—though at times it warms, depending.

Student: Depending on what?

Father: Well, it's a little... awkward to say.

Student: Say it, Dad.

Father: Sometimes you feel a little of this; sometimes you feel a little of that.

Student: An elder's way depends on this and that? So if elders guide rule, rule depends on feeling this and that?

Father: My point is this. If you can't see how everything all depends, you should never rule.

Student: What are we even talking about?

Director: I think we're talking about ruling others. Because surely, Father, you think we all should rule ourselves.

Father: Not if we're blind. People like that need to be ruled, without and within.

Director: I understand ruled without. But ruled within? How?

Father: Through religion and the like.

Student: And the like? What's like religion?

Father: Systems of belief.

Student: I might have had a lot to say about life-without-rule. But I wasn't proposing a system of belief.

Father: I know you weren't. And maybe that's the problem.

Director: How do systems of belief rule others within?

Father: Isn't it obvious? Others just have to accept the system. Then the system rules what they do from within.

Director: But the people have to believe. Isn't believing like that a form of self-rule?

Father: We can call it that. But in truth it's not. To rule your own self differs from importing belief.

Director: We need to make our own system?

Father: That's what the best of us do. No system of belief from others ever really fits just right. We can be our own tailor in this, and make our own clothes.

Director: Do we share what we wear?

Father: There's not much point in it. It's not one-size-fits-all.

Student: But then how do we know our system is right?

Father: We know by results.

Student: The results of a lifetime of belief?

Father: Yes. But we can, and should, make adjustments along the way. This is hard—but needs to be done.

85

Student: How do we know we're not just adjusting because the going got tough?

Father: Well, that's a problem. You have to trust your instincts here.

Student: But what if your instincts are bad? Or do you think it's human nature to have good instincts, and it's just hard to find and follow them here?

Father: Here's what I think. Each person has instincts that are hard to find and follow, yes. But not each person's instincts are good.

Director: There are good and bad natures.

Father: Yes.

Director: And this is from birth.

Father: It is.

Director: And no amount of nurture can make a bad one good.

Father: No amount. It might fool some people some of the time, but the true color will eventually show through.

Director: Can certain people develop an ability to see that color from the start?

Father: I have that ability. I'm rarely fooled. And when I am, I quickly recover and make corrections.

Director: You could vet people for Student's life-without-rule.

Father: I thought we were done with that.

Director: It seemed that way. But now an important possibility has opened up.

Student: I would like to learn this skill from my father then choose the people myself. After all, it should be my responsibility. I'm the one who needs to know. So how is it done?

Father: I'm not sure it can be taught. It's just something you feel in your bones. I don't know how I know. I just know.

Student: How is that different than my saying I just somehow know people aren't evil; it's that rule gets in the way?

Father: The difference is that I have to decide. You simply trust. You exercise no judgment here.

Director: But judgment as you describe it is a mysterious thing. We don't know why we judge. We just judge.

Father: Oh, it's not as bad as all that.

Student: Of course it is!

Father: Over time you get a feel for the signs.

Director: So Student just lacks experience?

Father: It's not quite as simple as that. If that were the case, every ninety-year-old on the planet would be an excellent judge of character.

Director: Then what's the trick?

Father: It is experience. But a certain kind of experience. Experience in judgment. You have to decide, then live by your decision.

Director: Unless you're wrong. Then you correct.

Father: Yes.

Student: But everyone has to decide about others then live by that decision. There's no avoiding this fact of life.

Father: But there is. Many people refuse to judge one way or another. They live their lives in a constant state of limbo. It's hard to decide about people and then move on. Not too many can do it.

Director: I don't know, Father. In my experience many people judge and move on all the time. The state of limbo you describe is rare.

Student: I think it depends on the person being judged.

Director: Can you say more?

Student: Some people are easy to judge. They wear their heart on their sleeve. Yes, you have to probe to make sure it's not an act. But once you're sure, you can decide—and live by your decision.

86

Director: Is it good or bad to wear your heart on your sleeve?

Student: I don't know. It just is. It does make it easier to judge. Some rotten people are right up front. So are some of the very good.

Director: Is wearing your heart on your sleeve somehow easier, easier on the wearer?

Student: Because it involves less inner rule? I think that's true in a way. But it's also harder because being that way can bring on unwanted consequences.

Director: And so some people believe tucking your heart away, having rule over your heart, is better. In other words, rule beats no rule here.

Student: Yes. And if people weren't bad because of life-under-rule, we would have no need to tuck our heart away. We'd be free to share.

Director: So when people are bad, we need more inner rule. And when people are good, we need it less.

Student: I think that's fair to say. After all, that's why we're more open with friends.

Director: Is there ever rule between friends?

Student: True friends? Never.

Director: Are true friends rare?

Student: Very, in life as we know it now.

Director: But when they're together, a sort of anarchy prevails—a little bit of life-without-rule.

Student: And that's why people believe life-without-rule would be good. They've had a taste and like it. Father?

Father: We rule ourselves with our very good friends more than we do with anyone else.

Student: But why?

Father: Because there's more at stake. Friendship is a precious thing. We are on our best behavior here.

Student: My best behavior is when I'm free. When are you free?

Father: In this life we're never fully free.

Student: Never? Dad, that's very sad.

Father: The fact that you feel that way tells me your sense of honor has yet to form. We take pride in standing up well to what the world throws our way. And lack of freedom is the hardest pitch.

Student: So when you were listening to me talking about life-without-rule, you were thinking I couldn't be more wrong.

Father: Yes. And I still do. But I have hope.

Student: Why?

Father: Sometimes the best of us need to go all the way over to truth's opposite extreme in order to get our bearings.

Director: And when they realize where they are?

Father: That's when they learn true inner rule. They have to fight their way back home. And as any true fighter knows, you never win the really hard fight unless you're squared away within.

Student: So I have to rule my heart. What else?

Father: You must rule your desires.

Student: How?

Father: You don't always act on them.

Student: How will I know when I can act?

Father: Ah, that's the art of life. You must develop a strong sense of prudence, Son.

Director: There is no prudence in life-without-rule, is there?

Student: No, there isn't. People have good desires and they act on them.

Father: But even with good desires, in the world as it is, you have to take care. People will try to get in your way, if only out of spite.

Student: It sounds like they need to rule themselves, not me.

Father: I know what you mean. But that's how it is. They'll rule you if they can.

Director: We have to rule ourselves in order not to be ruled by others. Rule or be ruled.

Father: Yes, but the saying usually has a different meaning. Rule others or be ruled by them.

Student: I don't want to rule others.

Father: Sometimes you don't have a choice. Sometimes it comes to this—rule them or be destroyed.

Student: I don't believe it. I'll just get away from them.

Father: Sometimes there's nowhere to go. You have ties to the place you're in. Family, friends, a job, whatever. You have to stand your ground.

Student: I'll stand my ground but I won't rule.

Father: You'll only make it harder on yourself.

Student: How? Isn't rule...the hardest job there is?

87

Father: Well, there's truth in that. You have to keep people in their place. There's nothing harder.

Student: But people don't like 'their place'—because it isn't their true place.

Father: Yes, that's true. Only they can find their own true place. If they had, they wouldn't be bothering you. But look. Sometimes being put in your place spurs you to find your true place. And that's the best you can hope for them.

Student: What can I hope for me? That one day I'll be able to set ruling others aside?

Father: You'll be ruling others until the day you die. It's necessity. There's nothing to be done.

Student: Director, do philosophers rule?

Director: I think it varies from philosopher to philosopher. Speaking in my own case, I do rule many of my desires. And there are people I rule at work.

Student: Why do you have to rule them?

Father: Why do you assume he doesn't want to rule them?

Student: Because Director is not that sort of man.

Father: What sort of man?

Student: The sort that rule gives a sense of importance. And perhaps a sense of security, too.

Director: Tell us, Student. Who makes the better ruler? The one who wants to rule, or the one who has to rule?

Student: The one who has to rule.

Director: Why?

Student: Because he or she has the clearer view. It's not clouded by desire.

Director: Does desire always cloud?

Student: No. But it does when it comes to rule.

Director: What is it about rule that makes desire, an innocent thing, bad?

Student: Rule interferes with other people's lives.

Father: Oh, we interfere with other people's lives just by walking down the street. But in a way, rule is quite considerate.

Student: How so?

Father: When you rule, you focus on the ruled and not yourself.

Student: Why would you do that?

Father: Otherwise you won't be effective.

Student: You mean you won't get what you want.

Father: Yes. But there's a trick. While focusing on them, you can't lose sight of yourself.

Director: Hmm.

Student: What is it?

Director: I just remembered we said rule is the imposition of will. My will doesn't dominate those I direct at work.

Father: But they do what you say. Right?

Director: Sometimes they persuade me to change my mind. But usually I persuade them.

Student: You can rule by persuasion not dominance.

Director: Father, what do you think?

Father: Persuasion differs from rule. Rule is dominance. You can cloak the dominance. But it's dominance, nonetheless.

Director: Why cloak the dominance?

Father: Most people don't like to be dominated. Or rather, most people don't like to think of themselves as dominated. It helps if you don't throw it in their face.

88

Director: Why do people like to be dominated?

Father: Who can say?

Student: Why can't the dominators limit themselves to dominating those who like it?

Father: This is the trouble with rule. The dominators can't limit themselves like that.

Director: Can we help them?

Father: The dominators? We can. They need to be ruled.

Director: How can we rule them?

Father: We have to be very strong. And let me tell you—it's exhausting.

Student: Too bad we can't rule them from within with a system of belief. We could channel all their energies for the good.

Director: What good do you have in mind?

Student: It would be wonderful if we could harness them to help create life-without-rule.

Director: How would that be possible? After all, rule is what they want. Do we trick them somehow?

Student: Why not?

Director: You'd really establish life-without-rule by fraud?

Student: It's better than by force. And there's a delicious irony here. So how do we do it?

Director: Maybe we convince them that monarchy is best, and that if they pick the right king, they will all assist in rule from within the innermost circle.

Student: And the king they pick is... you!

Director: I was thinking it would be you! Anyway, the monarch will follow our earlier plan for transitioning to life-without-rule.

Father: You'd have to kill all those of that innermost circle, you know.

Student: That would be our original sin.

Director: Is there any other way?

Student: Not that I can think of. The people would rejoice at their death, because you know they would have been tyrant-like in their limited rule. This would shore up support for the monarch. And then when he or she gives all the power away? Everyone is free.

Father: With many bad habits to break.

Student: Habits are easy to break when the reasons for them are gone.

Father: And you really think all bad habits stem from rule.

Student: I do.

Father: Say more.

Student: Rule crushes the spirit, even moderate rule. The spirit isn't meant to be ruled. Nor is it meant to rule. It's meant to be free. Give people a taste of freedom and watch them cast bad habits aside as though they never were there.

Father: Here we go again. Director, what do you say?

Director: I'm not going to say the human spirit, the human soul, is meant to be enslaved. Who doesn't believe it's meant to be free?

Student: Father?

Father: Oh, you're not going to get me to say we're meant to be enslaved. But there is freedom without and freedom within. We all should have freedom within. And we should have a large dose of freedom without—tempered, of course, by rule.

Student: Why should freedom be tempered?

Father: Because left untempered people run wild.

Student: People run wild as an equal and opposite reaction to rule. It's physics. Leave them free long enough and you'll see them settle down.

Father: How long is long enough? Years?

Student: How can I say for certain? But I think it's less than years.

Father: Even days of license can be very bad! Haven't you heard of the terrible times that follow the collapse of regimes?

Student: I have.

Father: Then you know that's to be avoided at all costs. Don't you?

Student: I don't want a collapse. I want a quiet fading away. A gentle transition would be best.

Director: Through your anarchic king?

Student: We would work with him to make the transition smooth.

Director: What about those who press?

Student: They don't understand what they're doing. This is a delicate affair.

89

Father: You don't know how glad I am that you call for gentleness here. At least you have sense enough in that.

Student: Gentleness is the hallmark of anarchy.

Father: Oh, that word still sounds so bad. I don't think you'll ever be able to shake its negative connotations.

Director: Is that something you'd like?

Father: What does it matter what I'd like? Life-without-rule is nothing but a dream.

Student: But is it a dream you share?

Father: Who wouldn't like a world where you live in peace?

Student: And happiness.

Father: And happiness. But you know my fear. We long for life-without-rule and instead we get anarchy-in-the-bad-old-sense.

Student: That's why we'll take our time and go gently. If we see signs of anarchy-in-the-bad-old-sense, we'll have to rethink.

Director: But what about that equal and opposite reaction you described? Won't that seem like anarchy-in-the-bad-old-sense?

Student: Running a little wild isn't the same as terrible anarchy.

Father: Oh, now it's 'a little' wild. Wild is wild.

Student: We won't let everyone have life-without-rule at once. We'll ease our way in. That way we can handle the shock.

Director: How do we choose who goes first?

Student: We start with the ones we think will go least wild, to establish a steady base.

Director: Who will go least wild?

Student: Those who are least oppressed by rule.

Director: And who are they?

Student: There is no simple answer. We have to interview them and decide.

Director: What are we looking for?

Student: Resentment.

Director: Against rule?

Student: Yes.

Director: And we choose those who have it least?

Student: Of course. With them there will be very little equal and opposite reaction, very little running wild, in the new world.

Director: And when we've sent them to life-without-rule we wait a while for them to get established then send the next bunch with slightly more resentment?

Student: Yes, exactly. And so on, until we get to the very worst. But by the time we come to them we will have a strong enough base to support them until they calm down.

Father: And then we live happily ever after.

Student: Why do you mock?

Father: Because I'm oppressed by rule. Why else?

Director: Student, when would I be sent to life-without-rule?

Student: Director, you would be among the first. I sense very little resentment, if any, in you.

Father: Did you ever feel it, Director? Maybe when you were young?

Director: I felt many things when I was young. Resentment toward rule may have been one.

Student: Oh, I'm sure you felt it. Anyone capable of independent thought has felt it. But how did you get over it? Did you focus on your inner freedom?

Director: I've always kept an eye on my inner freedom. But I've always kept two eyes on my outer freedom.

Father: Three eyes! Ha, ha. That's good. But you make a good point. You can't think yourself free. That happens outside.

90

Student: How?

Father: People will rule you as much as you let them. You have to take steps to prevent their rule.

Student: What steps?

Father: You have to make yourself strong so you won't be pushed around.

Student: Yes, but not all rulers push. Some of them pull. And there's more than one type of pull. Some will grab hold of you and tug, yes. That's what cavemen do. Others are more sophisticated.

Director: How?

Student: They have allure—and know how to use it.

Director: You mean like magnetic force?

Student: Yes.

Father: You're talking about something akin to love.

Director: Student, will there be magnetic pull in life-without-rule?

Student: Well, there will be love. But pull, as a sort of rule? No way.

Director: Where do you think the allure comes from, when it comes?

Student: Fascination with power.

Director: Power attracts.

Student: For those in life-under-rule, yes.

Director: What's wrong with being attracted to power?

Student: Power isn't attracted back. It may seem that it is, but that's because it wants to rule, to exploit you.

Director: And there is no exploitation in life-without-rule.

Student: None.

Father: And so we see, once again, that we're going to live happily ever after. All human badness will be gone.

Director: Student, do you think we'll one day forget all about rule?

Student: That would be a truly wonderful thing.

Father: You don't want people to learn from past mistakes?

Director: Maybe he doesn't want people to get any ideas.

Father: Well, they'll have all the old history books for that.

Director: Will they? Student?

Student: I don't see the point of having them.

Father: What? You'll burn all the old books and just have revisionist trash?

Student: I don't know that we'd have to burn them. People just won't want them anymore. In fact, they'll find them impossible to understand.

Father: But it's our past!

Student: We don't need that past anymore.

Father: This is a rotten thing. Director, what do you say?

Director: I say the past can be both entertaining and a cautionary tale.

Student: But these books won't mean anything to us.

Father: You never know who might profit from the books. Unless you think the ideas within are... dangerous.

Student: No, I don't think there's any danger here.

Director: Why not have the old histories serve as a test?

Father: Ha, ha. If you like the books, you're banished! But I do think the books can serve an important purpose.

Student: What purpose?

Father: They might one day help someone find a way out.

Student: A way out?

Father: Suppose anarchy takes root and flourishes for a while. But then there are problems, grave problems, problems you can't solve. The books would provide a guide for return to rule.

Student: That will never happen.

Father: Best to pack a parachute when you fly. And if you ask me, you're flying pretty high.

91

Student: With some things, the higher you fly the better you see.

Father: Then you should see what's necessary here.

Student: What's necessary?

Father: Your life-without-rule, if it's to stand a chance, needs to be life-without-rule-except-for-one.

Student: Not an executive again.

Father: Someone to guide the anarchy, to keep it from harm.

Student: Someone to rule.

Father: Yes.

Student: Then what's the point of the anarchy!

Father: Oh, take it easy. You need someone who can sniff out elements of rule—and act.

Student: How 'act'?

Father: Annihilate them.

Student: Director, what do you think of all this?

Director: Your father is saying it's purity versus success.

Student: I think that's a false choice. Life-without-rule purifies itself. It doesn't need a benevolent ruler for this.

Father: Yes it does—if you're wrong about human nature.

Student: If I'm wrong then all bets are off.

Director: So you'd have to settle for a type of rule?

Student: Yes.

Father: What type?

Student: It depends on the circumstances.

Father: How about our circumstances today?

Student: A democracy.

Director: Tomorrow?

Student: That's what depends.

Director: On how corrupt the democracy is?

Student: Yes.

Director: What makes a democracy corrupt?

Student: Corrupt individuals, if they're the majority.

Director: What then?

Student: We have to stop their rule.

Director: How?

Student: By whatever means.

Director: What makes an individual corrupt?

Student: They give in to rule.

Director: What are the signs?

Student: A certain sort of slavishness. They're the opposite of free.

Director: Do the free have pride?

Student: They no doubt do.

Director: And the slaves?

Student: If we're not talking about literal slaves, but the slavish? They lack all pride. That's what makes them slaves.

Director: What does pride allow you to do?

Student: Stand firm for what you know is right. The slavish never do that.

Director: Do the people in life-without-rule have pride like this?

Student: They... don't. They have pride. But not like this.

Director: Why not?

Student: Pride like that is in opposition to something. In life-without-rule, that something isn't there. Instead, we take pride in our way of life.

92

Director: Student, to get this way of life started, might it not be necessary to have a certain amount of rule?

Student: Well, possibly.

Director: Who would be worthy of this rule?

Student: That's the problem. No one is worthy of rule.

Director: But if we had to choose?

Student: It would be someone who holds rule highly suspect.

Father: Suspect of what?

Student: Being bad.

Father: So why would they rule?

Student: They'd have no other choice.

Father: They're forced to rule?

Student: Yes, but more by their conscience than anything else.

Father: So, what, one day we tell them it's time to rule, and that's it?

Student: We have to educate them toward a very limited rule.

Director: How do we choose the ones to educate? I mean, all who favor life-without-rule hold rule suspect. How do we decide?

Student: I... don't know.

Father: Oh, certain natures excel. Those are the ones you need.

Director: So an excellent one rules for a while and then they're relieved. But to be clear, what do they provide?

Father: Law, order, and security.

Student: But those in life-without-rule don't need law; the laws of human nature will suffice. They'll order their community on them.

Director: So law and order are covered. What about security?

Student: Who dares to attack a land of armed free women and men, each of whom are fully willing to die to preserve what they have?

Father: You expect me to believe that those unaccustomed to rule would gladly submit to military discipline if the need arose?

Student: You think those without rule don't know discipline? They impose it daily on themselves.

Director: Why?

Student: Because they see the benefits. That's why.

Director: And the lazy or cowardly?

Student: People are lazy when they can't see the worth of not being so. The same holds for cowardice. Our people will see. It's only natural that they do.

93

Director: Tell me something, Student, something we touched on before. Is it really possible to have less rule in a monarchy than a democracy?

Student: It all depends on the king or queen.

Father: But if they rule less, won't their regime be less secure?

Student: Not necessarily. People might be grateful for less rule. Their gratitude keeps the regime secure.

Father: But gratitude can change in the blink of an eye.

Student: Then the ruler should give no cause to blink.

Father: And what of the ruler's government, those who administer the state?

Student: If they give cause to blink, they must be removed—at once.

Director: What about aristocracy?

Student: It's to hard to have little rule in an aristocracy. The aristocrats compete. That competition drives up the amount of rule.

Director: Could they compete in having the least amount of rule?

Student: The first to go least will be conquered by their peers.

Director: But won't the people love them for their lack of rule? Won't they be loyal? Won't they be willing to fight to preserve them?

Student: Sure, but the other aristocrats will come with overwhelming force.

Director: What if we could get several aristocrats to conspire? You're in favor of very little rule. Might they not be, too?

Student: I suppose that's possible. But it's much easier with a monarchy.

Director: Yes, but there's something I've been wondering. If the monarch gives his or her power away, that power goes somewhere, no? Or does it just disappear?

Student: Well....

Father: Of course it goes somewhere, to someone. And the best we can do is dilute that power by spreading it out among many.

Student: You have a point.

Father: So democracy is best.

Student: Provided the government doesn't hold power aloof.

Director: What do you mean?

Student: Power the people can't touch by normal means.

Father: What are you talking about?

Student: Think of our Supreme Court. By design it's isolated from politics.

Father: Isolated? Hardly.

Student: Insulated, then.

Director: Would you take its power away? And if so, where would the power go?

Student: At best? To the private sphere.

Director: Hmm.

Student: What 'hmm'?

Director: Where is rule more intense? In the public or private sphere?

Father: I'll answer this. Rule is rule. But it might be better in government hands.

Student: You really think that? Why?

Father: Because there's more distance between you and the government than there is between you and the private sphere.

Student: Not always.

Father: No, not always. But when and where there is, I choose that. I need my space.

94

Director: The effect of rule diminishes with distance.

Father: Of course it does.

Director: What does that mean for our ever shrinking world?

Father: Between travel and communications technology the world is very small indeed. That means the effect of rule intensifies.

Student: I don't know about that. There has always been rule, even without technology like today. That rule was often intense.

Father: Yes, but you could get away from it if you really tried. I think that's harder today.

Director: So if we can't have life-without-rule, we at least need more distance.

Father: Mars isn't looking so bad.

Student: There was a company that opened up applications for a team that was to go on a one-way trip to Mars. Did you see how many people applied?

Director: I remember that. Many applied. But what happened to the company?

Student: It didn't get the funding it needed.

Father: Not enough people believed.

Student: No, I think plenty of people believed. But not enough very rich people believed.

Director: Why do you think they didn't?

Student: I suppose there wasn't enough profit for them.

Director: But the many people who applied didn't care about profit.

Student: No, they didn't. They cared about something more. Freedom and adventure.

Director: What if it were just one or the other? Would they believe if they were promised freedom alone? Adventure alone?

Student: People long for those things even on their own.

Director: Which is the greater longing? For freedom or adventure?

Student: It has to be freedom.

Director: Why?

Student: We can live without adventure, but we can't truly live without freedom. I do think, however, freedom often brings adventure.

Director: How so?

Student: Freedom, in a world of rule, involves danger. Danger and adventure are kin.

Father: Listen to you talk about danger. What danger have you known?

Student: Well... there is one experience....

Director: Don't be shy. Tell us.

Student: In the democracy class, there's a sense of danger. It makes things exciting.

Director: Does everyone feel excitement?

Student: No, I don't think so. I think some of the students are afraid. In fact, I think they feel oppressed.

Director: Oppressed? By some free talk?

Student: What can I say? They're cowards.

95

Director: Would these same cowards feel oppressed by the freedom of life-with-out-rule?

Student: There's a good chance they would.

Father: I thought life-without-rule cured all ills.

Student: It cures them by removing rule. But there is an inner rule it can't reach.

Director: What inner rule?

Student: The rule of fear. These people let fear rule.

Father: But do they have a choice? No one says, 'I think I'll let my fear rule.'

Student: They don't say it, but that's the choice they make.

Director: Interesting. In all our talk of life-without-rule, this is the first time we're speaking of choice. Everything else seemed to happen on its own. Are there other choices we're neglecting to mention?

Student: No, I think this is it.

Director: Do we kick out people who let their fear rule?

Student: The question is, why would they want to stay?

Father: You have a point. And it's for the best if they leave.

Student: To keep the community strong.

Director: I think we may have found the moral backbone of life-without-rule.

Father: Courage as the essence of morality. I like it.

Director: So, Student, is anarchy amoral or does it have a morality founded on this?

Student: Can all of us choose to have courage?

Father: No, some people are simply born cowards. No matter how hard they try, they'll show their true colors in the end.

Director: Can't some be born cowards while many are born with a choice?

Student: Of course. And maybe some are simply born brave. But I think, regardless of why the cowards are the way they are, we have to kick them out. There *is* a moral requirement for living life-without-rule.

Director: Are we sure life-without-rule can't eventually make the cowardly brave?

Student: Not if they don't let go of their fear. Some can't be cured.

Director: What about the young?

Student: What about them?

Director: Do we have to teach them morality, instill it in them?

Student: Well, if courage is a choice, maybe we should help them with that choice, educate them on that choice.

Director: But then is their choice... free?

96

Father: Children can't make a free choice.

Student: Of course they can.

Director: Do we judge them by what they choose?

Student: What do you mean?

Director: If some prove cowardly, do we weed out the weak?

Student: Hold on. I never said that.

Director: You don't think cowards are weak?

Student: I....They're kids!

Director: Let's say they're adults. Weed out the weak?

Student: We... should.... Some of the strong are cowards at heart, you know.

Director: I do know. Bullies and such.

Student: Exactly.

Director: We'll weed *them* out, right?

Student: Of course.

Director: Is there anyone else we'll weed out?

Student: No, I don't think so.

Director: So life-without-rule is the home of the brave.

Student: Each epoch needs its home of the brave.

Father: We have ours now. Don't be so quick to wish it away.

Student: If it can be wished away, it's already gone.

Director: Can there be more than one?

Father: There can be only one home of the brave.

Director: Student?

Student: It's not impossible for there to be more than one. If it were impossible, then things would have gotten very bad in democracy for life-without-rule to appear.

Father: I hope we never live to see the need for your life-without-rule.

Student: There's always a need for life-without-rule. People long for its freedom.

Director: Everyone longs?

Student: Maybe cowards don't. Or, maybe they do.

Father: I doubt it. I'll tell you what many of them long for—excitement.

Student: What do you mean?

Father: They find excitement in things like gambling, drinking, and drugs. Will you have those things in life-without-rule?

Student: No one will want these things. Living life will be excitement enough.

Director: But surely they'll have exciting recreations.

Student: What do you have in mind?

Director: Sports.

Student: There's nothing wrong with sports.

Father: But someone has to win.

Student: So?

Father: So someone will lose. Hard feelings might arise. And those who win might come to long to win again and again. They might become driven. Do you want driven people in your world?

Student: No, I think that's unhealthy and not a natural thing.

Father: Well, look at kids. Some of them just want to be first, to be best—from a very young age. What do you make of that?

Student: I don't think we'll see that when there's no rule.

Father: But if you do? Banishment again?

Student: We'll recognize it early on and gently curb them of the habit.

Director: And if it rears its head in adults?

Student: They're driven to be first in everything all the time? Banishment.

Director: Do you banish the whole family, or just the offender?

Student: Why would we banish the whole family?

Director: Because it's not a good idea to wound them then leave them in place. Chances are they'll long for revenge.

Student: Or be grateful we solved their problem.

97

Father: You really think life-without-rule can overcome family ties?

Student: If they're bad family ties? Yes, I do.

Director: What's the difference between good family ties and bad family ties?

Student: Bad family ties are based on rule.

Father: The father who rules his household is bad?

Student: In life-without-rule the answer is yes.

Director: Even as a parent simply ruling a child?

Student: Parent's shouldn't rule. They should parent.

Father: Do you honestly think you can parent without a healthy dose of rule?

Student: I know this all sounds fantastical, but life-without-rule is unique. Humans are free to develop fully—gently straightened as children, of course. But free. None of us here knows this freedom except as a memory from when we were born. For just that instant we knew something true and real. And it can happen again. Why look at your father as a king?

Father: Yes, I'd like to know why.

Student: Your father in the end will be a friend. And I know people say that those who try to be friends with their children are courting disaster. But they never experienced life-without-rule. The very air you breathe is different there. Fathers were kings because they felt they had no other choice. I'm telling them there's a choice.

Director: But it only works if everyone around you is living life-without-rule.

Student: That's right. That's the tragedy of this all. If only everyone would be willing to take that step, would be willing to let go....

Father: What if you let go and no one else lets go? I'd say you're in for some trouble then. Don't you agree?

Student: You'll be branded an anarchist-in-the-bad-old-sense. Yes, and this is bad. But I really believe a time may come when a critical mass of people can take that step, can just let go—and live their true lives.

Director: Does this have to be a primitive sort of anarchy, or can we have modern technology?

Student: I'm not sure. Modern technology is all tied up with modern economics. Modern economics is a complicated form of rule. So we wouldn't have a technological economy the way we know it today. But I don't think there's anything wrong with technology, *per se.* I just don't know how it would all work.

Father: I'll tell you how it would all work. It would all fall apart.

Student: Maybe. But I have more trust in my fellow men and women than to think they'd let everything go to hell.

Director: I'm trying to imagine what your heaven would be.

Student: I've told you.

Director: Yes, but I'm thinking of practical things. For instance, would there be a city with a surrounding countryside, for industry, trade, and food? Or would there be no city, just farms? Or just city? What?

Student: I don't know. We'll do whatever makes sense.

Director: And if there are differences of opinion on that?

Student: We'll try to persuade one another with reasons. If that doesn't work, I don't see why we can't try different ways. We can learn from our mistakes.

Father: You'd take the trouble to build a city and then decide it was all a mistake?

Student: Like I said, we'll do whatever makes sense.

Father: With no hard feelings toward whomever made the mistake?

Student: Everyone knows it takes courage to try. The ones who make the mistake will be praised.

Father: But not as much as the ones who succeed. It's only natural, Son.

Student: There's nothing wrong with that.

Father: No, unless jealousies arise.

Student: Jealousy is a function of rule.

Father: Yes, yes. We all knew that's what you'd say. But there really can be no doubt—it's a function of heart.

Director: Student, will you kick the jealous out?

Student: Look, this place won't be perfect. But the bad feelings will be less intense because everything else is so good.

Director: I think that's about the best argument you can make. I'd like for my bad feelings to be less intense. Who wouldn't?

Father: What bad feelings have you got?

Director: I go through the full range of human emotions once every great cycle or so.

Father: Great cycle? Ha, ha. So do I. Some emotions more than others.

Director: Student, will your people go through the full range?

Student: Of course. They're human after all.

Father: You're sounding more and more human, Son. More realistic, though I still think you're mostly talking about a dream.

Student: There have been anarchies, real anarchies, you know.

Father: I'm sure there have. During the English Civil War, The French Revolution, The Russian Civil War, The Spanish Civil War; and in Albania, Somalia—just to name some of the notable ones.

Director: What are the ones you were thinking of, Student?

Student: The Free Territory in Ukraine, Revolutionary Catalonia, the Shinmin Prefecture—to name some of the larger ones. But there have been numerous small communities throughout history.

Father: And how did they turn out? Oh, wait. Since I've never heard of any of them, they couldn't have turned out all that well!

Director: Student, I've heard that there are anarchist societies in existence today. Have you thought of going to one and living the life a while to see what you can learn?

Student: I'm afraid they're all tainted by rule.

Father: These anarchists aren't pure enough for you?

Director: Don't be embarrassed. Is it true?

Student: I read everything I could find, and I talked to everyone who would talk. All of these societies have... problems.

Father: Ha! As if they wouldn't! Student, you can't take on the world and not have problems. Maybe you'd be better off if you don't take on the world.

Student: I don't care about taking on the world. Believe me, my preference is to be left in peace!

Director: Anarchy is essentially peaceful, isn't it?

Student: Emphatically so.

Director: So it's ironic that the word 'anarchy' connotes violent disorder.

Student: It's more than ironic.

Director: Why does anarchy often involve violence?

Student: Because it's not really anarchy. In the kind of 'anarchy' we're talking about, small bands of ruthless criminals come to rule.

Director: Then why do people call it anarchy?

Student: Because the rule of the criminals isn't legitimate, people don't recognize it as rule. They see the problem as a lack of rule. But it's rule nonetheless.

Director: Does illegitimate rule always lead to violence?

Student: Not necessarily.

Director: Why is some illegitimate rule violent and some not?

Student: If an illegitimate ruler comes to power with overwhelming force, he or she can impose a peace.

Father: Are you suggesting that in such a situation, in a failed state, it's best for people to back the most powerful criminal in order ensure he or she has overwhelming force?

Student: Yes.

Father: And then what? Hope the criminal learns to be king?

Student: Stranger things have happened.

Director: Barring overwhelming force, is it possible to establish life-without-rule within minor criminal rule?

Student: With enough force to defend ourselves, I think it's possible. Criminals avoid organized resistance when they can.

Father: Here you are talking of organization in life-without-rule again.

Student: Organization and rule are very different things. An anarchy can be very well organized when there's a need.

Father: Would someone be the general of your army?

Student: If we needed an army? Yes.

Father: And you see no conflict between leadership and lack of rule?

Student: None.

99

Director: Leaders in life-without-rule must lead by persuasion. No?

Student: Yes.

Father: There is no time to persuade in war. Orders must be obeyed.

Student: People will have very good reason to do what the leaders ask.

Father: Assuming they trust the leaders. Why will they trust?

Student: They can just tell.

Father: Ha! I think your people are going to have to know the leaders from before, before your life-without-rule. That's how they will trust.

Director: Student?

Student: Well, I suppose there can be misunderstandings born of unfamiliarity.

Father: So for life-without-rule to take root, you need a large enough band of those who already trust one another.

Director: Is that all it takes?

Father: Of course not. These people will also need a large enough variety of essential skills.

Student: What do you mean?

Father: When a water pipe bursts, you'll need someone who can plumb. And, of course, you'll need those who can farm. And you'll need a doctor for the sick. And where will you get your medicine? Will you make it yourself?

Director: Student, will you trade with the outside world?

Student: Well, the colony on Mars won't.

Director: Why not? What if you could export precious metals and such? Or were you still intending to go dark?

Student: I suppose we could trade—so long as a ruling desire for things doesn't take hold. But if life-without-rule is well established, people will be happy with what they've got and only want what they need.

Director: So trade is dangerous at the outset?

Student: Yes.

Director: In life-under-rule, what makes people long for things?

Student: Mostly? I think it's status, which is a kind of rule.

Director: So if I have a great big house, a fancy car, all the electronics anyone could want, and so on—this would give me great status, and afford me a kind of rule over those who have less.

Student: Yes. It's not a formal sort of rule. But it's rule, nonetheless.

Father: But no one has to pay attention to you.

Student: But they do.

Director: Why?

Student: Because they have a hole in their soul, a void.

Director: What kind of void?

Student: It's the place where, in life-without-rule, happiness sits. They try to fill it with things.

Director: Does it work?

Student: I can't believe you're even asking. Of course it doesn't work!

Director: It doesn't work for you or me. But maybe there are those for whom it does in fact work. Or are we all the same?

Father: I know people who have much and are very happy they have so much. People are different, Son. So I think you have to banish those who find happiness in things.

Student: Maybe there's nothing wrong with finding happiness in things. The problem is if you take it too far.

Director: And in your life-without-rule no one will take it too far?

Student: They won't. Taking it too far means distracting yourself from other more important things. And given the chance, no one sacrifices the more important to the less important. No one.

100

Director: Rule distorts the importance of things. Is that fair to say?

Student: I think that says it all.

Director: What if you live a life-under-rule and you try to clear up these distortions? What will happen to you?

Student: At best you're a prophet; at worst you're a fool.

Director: Better to go off and practice what you preach?

Student: That's always better, yes.

Director: But first you'd have to gather a following, no?

Student: Well....

Father: Well what? Are you going to go off into the desert all by yourself? You'll need friends if not followers.

Student: Friends, yes. We'll gather up enough friends to make a start.

Director: Tell us, Student. Will everyone be friends in your anarchy?

Student: It's a society of friends, yes.

Director: But some friends will be better than others?

Student: Naturally.

Director: And jealousies and so on won't be felt with terrible force?

Student: They won't. People will have better things to do with their time than sit and brood.

Director: How will new members be admitted? Or can just anyone come?

Student: I think we have to screen, as we've said.

Director: No cowards.

Student: No cowards.

Director: And we said we'll be on the lookout for resentment toward rule.

Student: We did.

Director: Is that enough? How else would we screen?

Student: We'll look for signs of rule.

Director: The effects of rule?

Student: No, the desire to rule.

Director: Isn't the desire to rule one of the effects of rule?

Student: You have a point.

Director: So we'll look for the effects of rule. But won't everyone coming from a life-under-rule have some of the effects of rule?

Student: They will.

Director: So you never let anyone in?

Student: We look for intensity. The very intense we don't let in.

Director: You only let in those mildly affected by rule.

Student: Right.

Director: Well, if you want a mild society, that's what you should do.

Student: Do you think it's better to let in the intense? What kind of society would that produce?

Director: I don't know. But I suspect the intense will grow less intense under life-without-rule. And as they cool down, they may produce wonderful things.

Father: What, like art? I would think they'll produce wonderful art while they're intense.

Student: But that presents a problem.

Father: What problem?

Student: The other artists who are already cool, they might...

Father: ...be jealous of the intensity?

Director: Why would they be jealous?

Student: The intense artwork might get all the attention.

Director: Because intensity is inherently better?

Student: It calls attention to itself.

Director: So what can we do?

Student: Keep the products of intensity tucked away.

Father: Tucked away? For whom to see?

Student: No one.

Father: Why not just burn them, Son?

Student: Because we want the artist that made them to come back one day and see them.

Director: Why?

Student: So they can chart their course from hot to cool.

Father: It seems an awful shame. Shouldn't everyone be able to chart this course? Or do you have something to hide?

101

Student: What's to hide? The torture of being hot? That would serve as a warning to all.

Director: So why not warn?

Student: Maybe... we should.

Father: Good. There will be some real art in your realm.

Student: The best art will no doubt be the cool.

Father: Let the people judge. I'm interested to see where they come down.

Director: Art as a test?

Student: Why not?

Father: Ha! You won't rule but you'll police people's tastes?

Student: Of course not. Art isn't really a test. It just helps us understand people better. It's an invitation to conversation.

Father: I'm not sure I'd want to take part in such 'conversation'.

Student: Oh, there's nothing sinister here. Honest conversation sparked by art. What's wrong with that?

Director: I think that's a healthy thing. It might help you work through festering problems in the community.

Student: Art can give language to those problems that otherwise go unnamed. That's what good art does.

Father: What if the art speaks in praise of rule?

Student: Let it. We'll see it for what it is, and maybe learn a thing or two of the effects of rule.

Director: And the artist will learn, too. No?

Student: Artists should always learn something from the reception of their work. The artist should be part of the conversation.

Director: So even bad art can serve a good purpose.

Student: Certainly.

Director: Anarchy is an open society.

Student: Decidedly, yes.

Director: And that means it will let anyone in, at least to visit?

Student: Well... no, not quite—as we discussed.

Director: We discussed hiding yourselves away. But what if you don't hide? Who won't you let in?

Student: People with violent tendencies.

Director: What about people who want to come in and rule?

Student: Good luck to them. No one would pay them any attention. There'd be no one to rule.

Director: So you'd let them in?

Student: I don't think so, at least not for long. If they spend all their time trying to rule, they contribute nothing to society.

Director: They'd be parasites.

Student: Yes.

Director: Then again, maybe they'd be like bad art. They might spark conversation.

Student: But would they learn?

Director: If you learn, you can stay? How do you know if someone has learned?

Student: They change what they do and say.

Father: Every great liar and actor is a great learner, then.

Director: Actors might bide their time until they can strike out and rule.

Student: That's a cancer within.

Father: So what will you have? Loyalty tests?

Student: Of course not. That's something rulers have. We'll be able to tell. You simply can't hide something like this for long. It gets to the core of who you are. And who you are seeps through.

Director: Always?

Student: If we're living true life-without-rule, always. Everyone will notice. It's only if we're corrupt that someone like this stands a chance.

102

Director: How does life-without-rule become corrupt?

Student: That's much as to ask how rule came about.

Director: Why?

Student: Because life-without-rule came first, then corruption brought rule.

Father: So answer the question. How did life-without-rule become corrupt?

Student: Through very bad luck. Failed crops, drought, floods, earthquakes, monsoons, tornadoes, foreign invasion, plague. You name it. After enough of that people are susceptible to rule.

Director: The ruler makes promises to improve the common lot?

Student: Yes.

Director: Does he or she?

Student: I believe the answer must be... yes.

Director: Interesting. Why?

Student: Because people would never let go of the beauty of life-without-rule if they weren't forced to opt for something that would improve their Fortune-crushed life. And once forced, it takes a very long time to get the beauty back.

Director: So rule isn't always bad.

Student: It's not.

Director: Well, Father, I think we've come a long way.

Father: Rule isn't always bad. Yes, that's a long way.

Director: Will the people in life-without-rule know this truth? It seems to me there is going to be a very strong prejudice against it.

Student: If so, we'll have to fight it.

Director: How?

Student: It will be hard. After all, they will be coming from a very advanced stage of rule—many generations after the flood, so to speak.

Director: Yes. They will have forgotten the necessity that was.

Student: Yes. But we'll remind them how it goes. It's beauty, very bad luck, necessity for rule, entrenchment of rule—and then the longing for beauty once again. They must know this truth.

Director: Tell me something. Do animals have rule?

Student: What, are you asking if rule is by nature?

Director: Is it?

Student: Well, bees have a queen.

Director: What about other animals?

Student: I suppose there's an alpha male to every pack.

Director: How about whales?

Student: I don't think we know enough about them to say.

Director: Do we know enough about any animals to say whether they live in a state of pure anarchy? Earlier you suggested we do.

Student: I would say there are some that do and some that don't. Animals aren't a homogeneous type.

Director: Some animals are better than others?

Student: Yes, just as some humans are better than others.

Director: Do anarchic animals belong with anarchic humans?

Student: That sounds about right.

Director: Hmm. What about cats?

Student: Have you ever tried to rule a cat?

Director: No, but I gather it's not very easy.

Father: It's impossible, that's what it is.

Director: You've tried?

Father: I knew better. You can just tell.

Director: So humans are weaker than cats? They can be ruled?

Father: Ha, ha. I suppose you have a point. Maybe the cat is the official animal of anarchy.

Student: Our flag will be a black cat on a field of green.

Director: Why a black cat?

Student: To flout the notion that it brings bad luck.

Director: Why on green?

Student: Green stands for nature and growth.

103

Father: The cat makes me think of Halloween.

Director: Halloween is a sort of anarchic event, isn't it?

Student: How do you figure?

Director: You can be whatever you want. There are hardly any rules.

Student: That's a fair point. In a sense, every day is Halloween in life-without-rule.

Father: Do you really think that makes your case stronger?

Student: People are afraid to be what they want in life-under-rule. They're afraid what people will say.

Father: The general will might go against them.

Student: Yes. In life-without-rule people don't have that fear. So they're free to be whatever they want.

Father: And no one will want anything bad because it's not in human nature to want anything bad.

Student: Bad means bad for you. No one wants that.

Director: Student, would you say that life-without-rule *without*, on the outside, requires life-without-rule *within*?

Student: Of course.

Director: So to be free without, to be whatever you want—you have to be free within.

Student: Right.

Director: And that means no rule within.

Student: Certainly.

Father: Really? No self-control?

Student: Why should you control yourself when nothing you want is bad?

Director: Father, can you imagine a life of such freedom?

Father: I honestly can't.

Student: You want bad things.

Father: What I want is my business alone.

Student: In life-without-rule what you want is everyone's business—so it can be fulfilled.

Father: Nonsense.

Student: Why?

Father: We all have bad desires.

Student: Such as desire for revenge?

Father: Yes, for one. Who will fulfill my desire for revenge?

Student: Maybe you wouldn't want revenge if you came to life-without-rule.

Father: Maybe.

Student: You can visit and see how we live, then decide if you want to stay.

Father: You're speaking as if your society already exists.

Student: I'm confident it will.

104

Director: Why are you so confident?

Student: Because nature is on my side.

Father: Here we are with the dream again. If nature is so on your side, why is there precious little evidence of any successful anarchy in all of human history?

Student: When anarchy existed, no one felt the need to record the fact.

Director: So history is the result of a fallen state?

Student: Yes. The first historians didn't know why they felt the need to record. The reason was a need to get at the roots of rule. That's what all history has been since. Now that we know the end, the goal toward which we strive, we see history for what it is—an artifact of the longing for life-without-rule.

Director: There's no need for history in life-without-rule?

Student: Why would there be? People won't do what they do in order to be written down in books. People will write, sure. But it won't be for the annals of all time.

Director: People really won't want life-surpassing fame?

Student: People really won't want life-surpassing anything.

Director: What a remarkable change.

Student: Indeed.

Director: But, in a way, I think life-surpassing fame can serve the cause of surpassing rule.

Student: How?

Director: The strongest longing for fame breaks the bonds of rule.

Student: Can you give an example?

Director: Founders of regimes. They break the old rule and long for fame as founders of the new.

Student: The Founding Fathers?

Director: Sure. They broke old Britain's rule.

Student: Can you imagine if they did that then set up life-without-rule?

Father: Britain would have conquered us very quickly then.

Student: How can you be so sure?

Father: I know how power works.

Student: Do you think that's why the Native Americans lost?

Father: What do you mean?

Student: Weren't they more anarchic in their way?

Father: They had many ways, and I have no idea.

Student: Director?

Director: I haven't made a study of their ways. We'd have to see.

Student: Well, I think today's Native Americans can see the benefit of life-without-rule more clearly than many.

Director: Why?

Student: They don't take part directly in the greater life-under-rule. They stand apart.

Father: I think you have to be careful here.

Student: How come?

Father: No group that I know of likes to be branded anarchist. They might resent you for it. And even if you're right, it calls unwanted attention to them.

Student: You're saying I should mind my own business.

Father: Yes. Go and learn from these people if you want. But let them worry about what they're called. It's none of your affair.

Student: I'm surprised you encourage me to go.

Father: I do because I think you'll find rule wherever you go. It might sober you up, focus you on more productive things.

105

Director: And if it doesn't sober him up?

Father: He becomes even more idealistic? I'll dry up the money.

Director: There are plenty of idealists who persist in poverty. In many cases, it strengthens their resolve.

Father: More fool them.

Director: In fact, some of the greatest idealists I've come to know come from money but live in poverty.

Father: Then let's not hope great things are in store for my son.

Student: Oh, you don't mean it. Don't you want me to do something with my life?

Father: I do. I want you to earn a living and build on this family's wealth. That's something you can do. Doing that should make you proud. And trying to do that will give you a real lesson in what human nature is.

Student: I have no doubt it's very hard for many to earn a living. But when you speak of amassing wealth you're really speaking of rule. You make it hard on yourself for the sake of rule. You could take it easy and rest content with what you have. But you want more. Why? Because the more you have the more you rule. Rule is like a very bad drug. It takes more and more to achieve the same effect, the high you come to crave. And you want this for me?

Father: Director, can you talk some sense to him?

Director: Student, is your father really a dealer who gets high on his own product?

Student: Would it be better if he didn't?

Director: What's the price he wants you to pay for this drug?

Student: My freedom.

Director: Why would a father want to take his child's freedom away?

Student: Because it's a threat.

Director: To him?

Student: To what he thinks of himself.

Director: What does he think of himself?

Student: He thinks of himself as free.

Director: And when he's confronted with what *you* take as freedom?

Student: It's beyond what he can take.

Director: I'd say you've been pretty free here today in our talk. Do you agree? Or is there more you'd like to say, something you've been holding back?

Student: I haven't been holding back.

Director: Your father seems to me to be taking all your freedom with us quite well. Has he raised his voice?

Student: No.

Director: Has he shown signs of anger?

Student: Anger? No.

Director: Has he made any threats?

Student: Well, he did say he'd dry up the money.

Director: But based on what you've said, can you say that's very surprising?

Student: No, I can't.

Director: There is one thing I wonder about. He laughed a few times. Did that upset you?

Student: It didn't make me feel good.

Director: Is a father bad if he doesn't always make his son feel good?

Student: That would be ridiculous to say.

Father: I'm sorry if I made you feel bad. As I've said, I too was young. And I'm very open when I say I think you'll grow out of all this. You just can't make any irreversible moves.

Student: Like what?

Father: Giving all your money away after I'm gone.

Student: I can't make any promises. I'll do what I need to do for the cause.

106

Director: Father, do you have a cause?

Father: My family is my cause.

Student: What's your cause, Director?

Director: I'm not sure I have one.

Father: If you're not sure, you don't.

Student: I think philosophy is your cause.

Director: What makes you say that?

Student: Every conversation I've ever had with you always comes around to philosophy.

Director: Well, maybe it's true.

Student: Why are you shy to admit it?

Director: Philosophy has taught me to be wary of causes.

Student: Why?

Director: Because they're often excuses to shut down thought.

Student: But when I talk about life-without-rule with others, it often spurs them to think.

Director: Yes, but what about you? Is it possible you're doing more believing than thinking?

Father: That's an excellent point. I've always known this about certain causes, but never put it in so many words.

Student: What thinking do you do about your cause?

Father: Try and raise children and support a family and tell me if you don't think. You sometimes think things you could never imagine.

Student: Are you better for this thought?

Father: Some of it, yes. But I'll be honest with you. Sometimes the thoughts aren't good.

Student: What do you do then?

Father: I drive them away and focus on the task at hand.

Student: And when you have, when you've completed the task?

Father: I usually feel much better.

Student: Director, does philosophy make you think bad thoughts?

Director: We all think bad thoughts at one time or another. Is it philosophy that *makes* me think them? I'm capable of doing that all on my own.

Student: In other words, don't blame philosophy. But look at you smile!

Director: It's rare that true philosophy doesn't take the blame.

Student: Why do you think that is?

Director: Tell me. When you preach life-without-rule, does everyone you encounter like to think as a result when you're done?

Student: Well, I don't preach. I converse. And no, not everyone likes to think as a result.

Director: Do some of them suppress their thoughts, thoughts your talk might have stirred?

Student: Yes, definitely.

Director: Do some of them resent you for making them have to suppress?

Student: I didn't make them suppress. They did that on their own.

Director: That's a good answer. So I take it you can understand how it goes with philosophy.

Student: I think I can.

Father: I think I have some idea, too. But, Director, even with all this talk, I know you have your priorities straight—because you have a responsible job. You direct the efforts of a large team. Philosophy is an admirable hobby for your time off. But why are you laughing, Son?

107

Student: Director doesn't think of philosophy as a hobby. He practices philosophy at work.

Father: I don't see how that's possible. Is it true, Director?

Director: It's true.

Father: But you know your job is more important than philosophy. Right?

Student: Oh, don't push him, Dad. Of course he knows. Otherwise how could he hold a job?

Director: Why do you put it like that?

Student: If you engaged in full bore philosophy all the time, you'd have no time for work.

Director: I really do work.

Father: So it's water cooler philosophy, right?

Director: Any time I have opportunity to engage in philosophical dialogue, I do. Sometimes this is at the water cooler; sometimes this is at my desk; sometimes this is in a conference room with many others present.

Father: But your kind of philosophy is conducive to business.

Director: That's been my luck so far.

Father: Oh, don't be modest. I can imagine the kind of conversations you have. You have young people on your team, don't you?

Director: I do.

Father: Do you converse with them?

Director: Yes.

Father: Do you think you make them think?

Director: They sometimes tell me I do.

Father: Then I'm certain you make them think more than they know. I think they owe you something for this.

Director: No, I think if they think they know why they think. And they don't owe anything to me. In fact, I probably owe them.

Father: What could you owe them?

Director: More of the truth than I give.

Father: Oh, you're too hard on yourself. No one can give the full truth. At least not under ordinary circumstances. And full truth always comes at a cost.

Director: You're intriguing me now. What cost?

Father: Sometimes when you share everything, one of you has to walk away.

Student: Director, is that true?

Director: Your father is more profound than I knew.

Student: But is it true?

Director: I don't know.

Student: How can you not know?

Director: It's happened that way with me. But I don't know if it was necessary.

Student: You mean it may have been a mistake?

Director: I suppose it remains to be seen.

Student: What does that mean?

Director: Maybe they'll one day return.

Student: So you weren't the one to walk away.

Director: Right. I've never walked away.

Father: Oh, that can't be true.

Student: Why not?

Father: Because sometimes when you share everything, or as close to everything as you can, you need to walk away.

Student: Why?

Father: Because there's nothing more to say. And you're not going to just stand there gazing into one another's eyes, forever.

108

Student: You said maybe one day the ones who walked away will return. What then?

Director: We'll be friends without rule.

Student: You'll seek to live life-without-rule?

Director: We won't have to seek. We'll be there.

Father: Director is right. The only true life-without-rule in this world is the rule-free time together with excellent friends.

Student: But I thought you said—

Father: Never mind what I said. We're speaking of something rare.

Student: Are you becoming... radical?

Father: Ha! Let's just say a little anarchy in life can be good.

Director: And it stands out all the more against a backdrop of rule.

Father: Yes.

Student: I think our talk today is an example of life-without-rule.

Director: Can you say how?

Student: You have no desire to rule either of us here. We have no desire to rule you. My father does try to rule me, but he suspended his efforts, mostly, today.

Director: So life-without-rule is possible in fleeting conversations?

Student: Yes, I think it is. It's extremely limited, but it's real.

Director: And is this possible anywhere private conversation can happen?

Student: Yes. It just takes bringing the right people to the table.

Director: How can you tell who the right people are?

Student: Oh, I think you can tell by how they interact with you in general. And if you're wrong, at worst, the conversation fizzles.

Director: What happens if more and more people start having free conversations like this?

Student: The world grows closer to life-without-rule.

Director: Why?

Student: Because when people know what's possible, they want more of it.

Director: So will you seek out people who don't seem inclined to rule and talk about life-without-rule with them?

Student: Yes, definitely.

Father: Oh great, the blind leading the blind.

Student: Tell me something, Dad. Did you enjoy our conversation today?

Father: Much of it.

Director: What didn't you enjoy?

Father: The parts that made me uneasy.

Student: Which parts?

Father: I think you can guess.

Director: He was uneasy when we spoke of things he believes require rule. It's dangerous to question here.

Father: Oh, don't make me out to be squeamish. It's fine to talk. But we have to recognize that it's nothing but talk. Sometimes radical talk points us to prudent ways.

Student: How is that possible?

Father: When you depict the limits of a thing, you also show what's possible within them.

Director: Is it always prudent to stay within?

Father: Sometimes you have to go beyond.

Student: When?

Father: When the house is on fire. But we have no fire today.

Student: None that you see. But look outside this country club we're in.

Father: There's always a fire someplace, Son. This place isn't so bad. Is it?

Director: Student seems to think it is.

Father: I should have made him work before he went off to college. He'd be less concerned with anarchy and more concerned with getting ahead.

Student: How do you know? Maybe rule at work would have made more radical.

Father: What more is there? You're out to undermine every institution there is! But I have to go. We'll talk about this again. Director, thanks for putting up with my son. Will your team have the paperwork ready for tomorrow?

Director: It's already ready. I'll send it to you first thing, or later tonight if you'd like.

Father: No, tomorrow is good. Son, you and Director should stay. Better you talk crazy with him than go back tonight and talk crazy with your peers. Spend the night at home and drive back early tomorrow. You'll do that, won't you?

Student: Of course I will, Dad.

Father: Good. I'll be home before dawn. We can have coffee and breakfast then. I'll look forward to that.

Student: So will I. We'll have much to talk about.

Director: About life-without-rule?

Student: Yes, what it means in very practical terms.

Father: Director, why do I get the sense he'll want me to surrender some of my paternal authority?

Director: Because he's all grown up.

Father: True. But—and forgive me, Son—he's not yet mature.

Director: The best way I know to help someone mature is to talk seriously about what weighs on their mind.

Student: I have a lot on my mind.

Father: Then I'm all ears.

Director: But don't hesitate to challenge him in what he says. You can't be mature unless you can handle a challenge well.

Father: Do you really think I won't challenge?

Director: I think you have a soft spot in your heart. You never would have stood for all we said today if you didn't.

Father: I challenged much of what was said.

Director: But you never silenced your son. And you, Student, I hope you understand what sort of father you have. Many would never have stood for open talk of anarchy.

Student: I do understand. Many of the students at school won't stand for it. They get very upset. The 'Questioning Democracy' class is controversial.

Father: As it should be. If it weren't controversial, I'd say something is very wrong.

Student: What would that mean, exactly?

Father: There's a fire burning close to home.

Director: How can we put it out?

Father: We can return to our roots, the things that made us strong.

Student: But there is no going back.

Father: Of course there is. You just have yet to see it happen.

Student: This is the real heart of the matter. Do we go forward into life-without-rule, or do we waste our efforts in a hopeless attempt to go back.

Father: This is the real heart of the matter. Do we chase some impossible dream while our house burns down, or do we fight the fire with proven methods?

Student: Methods must change with the times.

Father: I'll grant you that. But first we have to know the times. We can't do that with our heads in the clouds.

Director: It seems you'll have plenty to talk about tomorrow morning. Maybe you can get into particulars in the problems you see.

Student: All we have to do is look at the morning news and we'll have endless topics for conversation.

Father: Agreed. But now I really must go. Thanks for the stirring conversation—both of you. Like I said, I'll be home before dawn. These political meetings never seem to end. So, Student, don't wait up. I'll have coffee ready before you wake.

Student: I'll wait up. I have a lot to think about now. I can sleep when I get back to school. So I'll make the coffee when you get home. But when will you sleep?

Father: Once you're settled in a responsible job.

Student: Insomnia is bad for your health, Dad. Please don't put that on me.

Father: Director, can't you get him a job in your office?

Director: I might be able to manage that, yes.

Student: I'd be working with you?

Director: You would. Is that something you'd like?

Student: Yes! But only if you commit to bringing about life-without-rule.

Director: Let's take things a step at a time, and then we'll see what we think.

Father: Yes, Student, don't pull down the house on top of you.

Student: But I think that's what Director wants.

Director: I don't want to be caught in some collapse.

Father: You see? Director is no fool. So be grateful, and don't you fool with him.

Director: There's no fear of Student fooling with me—so long as he really wants to learn and know.

Student: Don't you think I do?

Director: I think there's a very good chance.

Father: Otherwise he never would have invited you in.

Student: But, Director, you say there's only a chance?

Director: What can I say? So many things can get in the way. And I've been wrong before.

Student: Then I will prove you right in hiring me.

Father: I can already see that things will go well. So maybe all this talk of anarchy will have not been for naught.

Director: It's never for naught when youth feels free to speak its mind.

Father: It's not for nothing, but there's no guarantee it's for something good.

Student: It's good when we learn.

Director: Father, have you learned today?

Father: Have you?

Student: I have. But now I'm intrigued to know if you two learned, and if so what.

Father: Let's talk about this tomorrow. And intrigue is good. It stimulates learning.

Student: It's too bad most teachers don't know this is true.

Director: It's too bad most teachers don't learn when they teach.

Student: You sound like my professor now.

Director: Maybe I'll come to class with you one day.

Student: That would be great!

Director: The professor wouldn't mind?

Student: No, not at all. He'd welcome you for sure.

Director: How do you know?

Student: He'll sense you have no desire to rule.

Director: And if I did?

Student: You'd watch in silence.

Director: Those who'd rule have nothing to say?

Student: Oh, they have plenty to say—but not in class.

Director: Why not?

Student: The atmosphere doesn't conduce.

Director: You want this atmosphere outside of class, too, don't you?

Student: I really do.

Director: Does the teacher know this about you?

Student: I don't know.

Director: Haven't you been in to talk to him alone?

Student: I haven't.

Director: Well, let's change that. If he'll have us, you and I will talk with him alone after class.

Student: He'll have us. How could he not?

Director: Good. I'd like to hear what he has to say.

Student: I think he'd like to hear what *you* have to say.

Director: And what about you?

Student: I'd rather listen to my elders and learn.

Father: That's a promising sign.

Student: Promising that I know to shut my mouth?

Father: As an anarchist, there are worse things you can do.

Student: What do you think might I learn?

Father: That your professor has it wrong.

Student: And Director has it right?

Father: Always remember—he has a responsible job.

Student: And my professor doesn't?

Father: He has tenure, this professor of yours?

Student: Yes.

Father: If that's not an invitation to be irresponsible, I don't know what is.

Student: You think he wouldn't teach anarchy if he weren't tenured?

Father: Not unless his department were filled with anarchists.

Director: But there also has to be a certain receptivity among the students, no?

Father: Well yes, of course—and that's a bad sign.

Student: It's a good sign, Dad.

Director: Let's talk to some of these students after our talk with the professor.

Student: Yes. We'll go to the coffee shop and sit down with some of them.

Director: Good.

Father: What will you say? 'Hello, I'm Director and I'd like to talk about rule'?

Director: I'll ask them what they thought of class and take it from there.

Father: But where will you take it? That's the question.

Director: I think the question is less where I'll take it and more where they'd like to go.

Student: You won't attempt to rule the conversation. It will be a talk like the one we had today.

Director: That's my hope. But, Student, you know that means I'll seek to disabuse them of any false hopes or beliefs they have about life-without-rule.

Student: But I will, too. I want them to have a true *view*.

Director: Then we know what we must do.

Printed in the United States
by Baker & Taylor Publisher Services